The Book of Independence.

They're intent on completing their round the world trip in 10 years and, possibly, to invent whatever excuse afterwards to remain in motion
Lonely Planet Magazine.

This overland autobiography will leave you laughing aloud, inspiring you to get out and experience another part of the world
-one that is well outside your comfort level.
Overland Journal Magazine.

Around the World
in 10 Years:
The Book of Independence

Overlanding Turkey, Syria, Jordan and Egypt

Pablo Rey

Translated by Joaquín Ayala

www.viajeros4x4x4.com
contact: viajeros4x4x4@yahoo.com - Facebook & twitter @viajeros4x4x4

Author: Rey Berri, Pablo Gustavo
Around the World in 10 Years: The Book of Independence
   1st. English Edition – United States, november 2012
   Translated by Joaquín Ayala

La Vuelta al Mundo en 10 Años: El Libro de la Independencia
   1st. edition – Barcelona, Spain, April 2010
   2nd. edition – Buenos Aires, Argentina, December 2010
   3rd. edition – United States, June 2011

Viajeros4x4x4 Editions
222 p.; 6" x 9" - 15,24 x 22,86 cm.
ISBN-13 978-1482769951
ISBN-10: 1482769956
Legal Deposit: B. 15.228 - 2010
1. Travel, Travel Narrative. I. Title

Cover Design: El Laboratorio, María José Baglivo and Pablo Rey
Photographs and Layout: Pablo Rey
Photographs of Anna and Pablo: Carlos Holemans Mestres

The unpublished soundtrack for this book includes songs by Creedence Clearwater Revival, The Doors, Joaquín Sabina, The Rolling Stones, Iggy Pop, The Smiths, Patricio Rey y Los Redonditos de Ricota, Ray Charles, U2, Bersuit Vergarabat, Maceo Parker, Michael Nyman, Maria Joao ...

AROUND THE WORLD IN 10 YEARS CONTINUES AT WWW.VIAJEROS4X4X4.COM

Dedicated to those who never give up.

Foreword

Halfway through the journey of my life
I found myself bewildered within a gloomy forest
For I had lost all trace of the right path.

So wrote Dante during the year 1300. Exactly 700 years later Pablo Rey also discovered he was in a gloomy forest and was in urgent need of finding the right path. Our paths crossed a dozen years later in a series of breathtaking synchronistic entanglements worthy of a meeting between Carl Jung, Salvador Dalí, and Hunter S. Thompson. It all began when some friends who are in the habit of helping and housing world-travelling Mitsubishi Delica drivers told me they had guests arriving who might be of interest. They, like me, were from Barcelona. The Spanish population in Vancouver, British Columbia is small. Smaller still is the Catalan community, so I quickly invited myself.

As part of the mysterious lattice of coincidence which follows me around, I was at this point through the journey of my life also looking to make great changes. Extended travel to obscure locations was at the top of the list. The disillusionment with many aspects of my gloomy daily routine was becoming unbearable, and clearly a different path was necessary. The event was a pot luck dinner, and I took along a large *tortilla* (potato omelette), some *pa amb tomàquet* (lightly toasted baguette smothered with tomato, drizzled with olive oil and sprinkled with salt) and some fine *Penedès* wine. After talking with Pablo and Anna about their travels and adventures, I bought their book and was quickly won over. Not only did the text resonate with much of what I believed, but remembering the places described in the book brought back many pleasant memories. I have always travelled light on my long-distance bicycling adventures, sometimes ridiculously so. Pablo and Anna have, also by accident and as described in the book, stumbled on the same counter-intuitive truth: the further you want to travel, the less you need to take. Much the same is true in life. I am struck by the similarities in our ways of thinking and of how they have made continual travel more than just a lifestyle choice but rather an art-form centred on the search for the right path.

The role of meaningful coincidence in our lives generated hours of late-night discussion and many empty bottles both in Vancouver and when I visited them in Barcelona. While we all have a healthy disbelief towards claims of the paranormal, the tendency to encounter just the right person with just the right skill-set at just the right moment to make just the right highly unlikely series of events unfold runs through much of this narrative. There are various plausible explanations for these seemingly highly improbably chance meetings, but even being well aware of the statistical reality does not reduce the magical quality of these events as they occur.

I decided the book deserved to be made available to a wider audience, and so undertook the translation into English. As much as possible I've tried to preserve the rhythm of the narrative, as I soon realized that for this book the cadence of the language was far more important than purely grammatical considerations. If the rules had to be bent, I would bend them. As a musician this made a great deal more sense to me and felt more comfortable when I read back the passages.

While this project took many hours to finish, it was far from a solo effort. Special thanks go to Christine Lambert for the many excellent suggestions when my translation seemed clearer to me than to her. Thanks also to Jay Willoughby for putting up with us as we endlessly debated the merits of a single word or phrase. Thanks to Lori Pappajohn and Pep Ventura for additional editing. Thanks also to Anna Callau for cooking us all some memorable Catalan meals before and after our extended proofing sessions, for much insight in clarifying some obscure points and subtleties in the text, and for the gentle humour. Finally to Pablo Rey himself whose questions during the reviews of my efforts often elicited the possibility of a different interpretation from what I had originally considered.

My hope is that with the publication of this book in English, a larger audience will consider the possibility that travel is not just something to do while on holiday. Rather, it's something far too important and necessary to postpone. For those lost within a gloomy forest, consider travel as a vocation, not merely a vacation.

Joaquín Ayala
Vancouver, Canada
April 2013

Index

Keep your dreams!
Madmen have sweeter ones than the wise!

Charles Baudelaire, Les Fleurs du Mal.

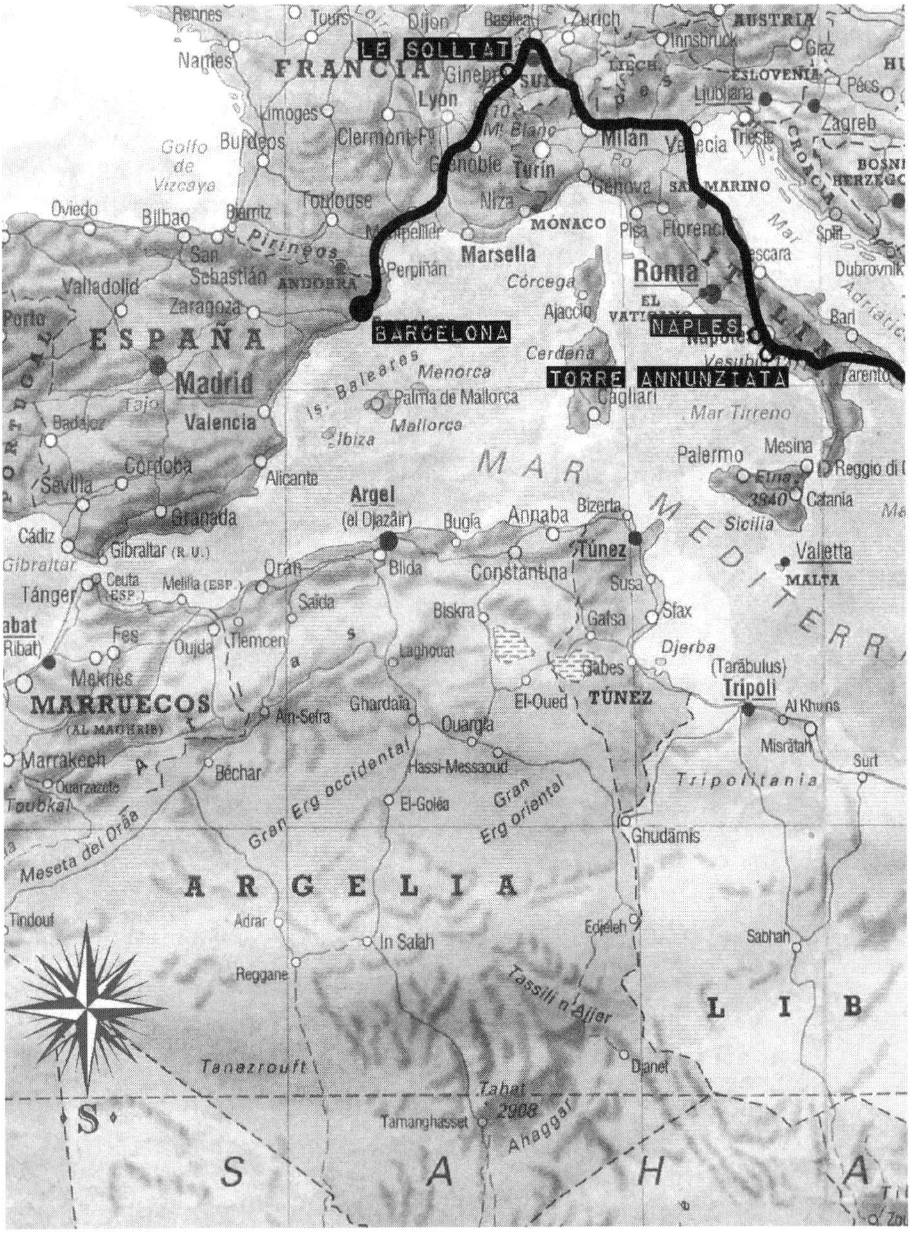
LE SOLLIAT
BARCELONA
NAPLES
TORRE ANNUNZIATA
FRANCIA
ESPAÑA
Madrid
Marsella
Roma
Argel
(el Djazâir)
Túnez
Tripoli
MARRUECOS
ARGELIA
Mar Tirreno
MAR MEDITERR
Sicilia
Cerdeña
Córcega
Menorca
Mallorca
Ibiza
Golfo de Vizcaya
Pirineos
ANDORRA
MÓNACO
SAN MARINO
EL VATICANO
AUSTRIA
ESLOVENIA
CROACIA
MALTA
Valletta
Gran Erg occidental
Gran Erg oriental
Tassili n'Ajjer
Tripolitania
Tanezrouft
S A H A
L I B

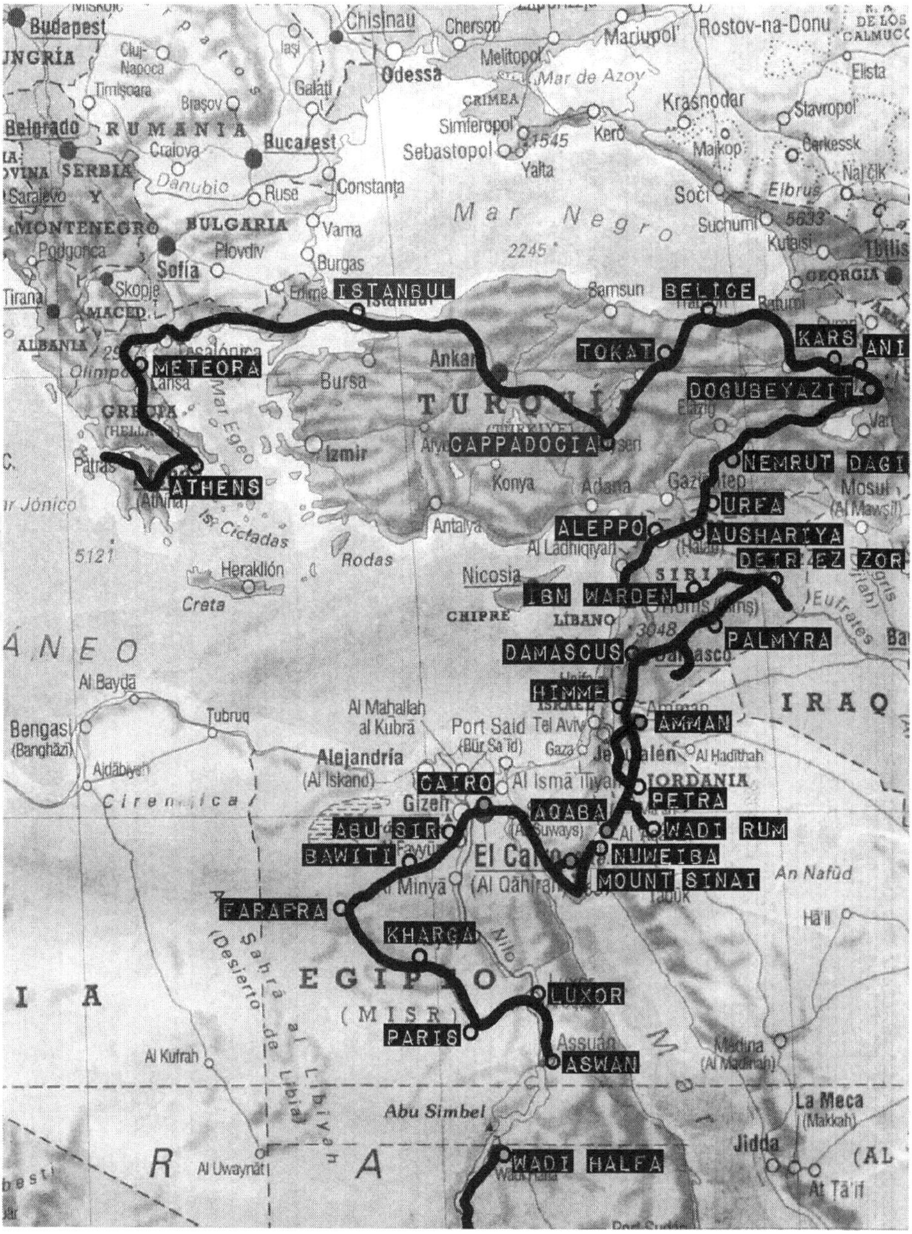
ISTANBUL
BELICE
METEORA
TOKAT
KARS
ANI
DOGUBEYAZIT
CAPPADOCIA
NEMRUT DAGI
ATHENS
URFA
ALEPPO
AUSHARIYA
DEIR EZ ZOR
IBN WARDEN
PALMYRA
DAMASCUS
HIMME
AMMAN
PETRA
CAIRO
AQABA
WADI RUM
ABU SIR
BAWITI
NUWEIBA
MOUNT SINAI
FARAFRA
KHARGA
LUXOR
PARIS
ASWAN
WADI HALFA
Budapest
Chisinau
Rostov-na-Donu
Odessa
Mar de Azov
RUMANIA
Bucarest
Krasnodar
Sebastopol
Constanța
Mar Negro
BULGARIA
Sofia
Tbilisi
Bursa
Izmir
Ankara
TURQUÍA
Konya
Adana
Antalya
Rodas
Cicladas
Heraklión
Creta
Nicosia
CHIPRE
LIBANO
IRAQ
Eufrates
Al Baydā
Tubruq
Bengasi
Alejandría
Port Said
Tel Aviv
Gaza
Jerusalén
JORDANIA
Gizeh
El Cairo
An Nafūd
EGIPTO
(MISR)
Nilo
Assuán
Abu Simbel
Al Kufrah
Al Uwaynāt
La Meca
Jidda

FREEDOM SMELLS LIKE COW DUNG

It's always the same story: as soon as you get used to the pace of your vacation, a phone rings. There's a call from God, Allah, Jehovah or your conscience reminding you that it's time to get back to work. Sometimes it's the same electronic buzz of your old cell phone that awakens you in a foreign land. But no, your phone is switched off. You promised.

In any case it startles you. That ringtone is yours, and your body responds like a faithful dog. Your hand slips unconsciously downwards, slowly falling towards your pocket. Pavlov would be proud. And you stop singing along to that new song you like and that's being played in the bars and radios of half the planet, *la-la du-bee du-doo*. Your brow begins to furrow. You reach for your phone and find a half-empty plastic container of suntan lotion.

The bitter flavour of melancholy, like bile, taints your mouth. For an instant you can taste your home town, and you don't like it. Your lot in life is not bad, but it sucks from this perspective. You look at your

Photo: The Sahara Desert near al-Qasr, Kharga Oasis, Egypt

swimsuit and further down to your feet, tattooed by a healthy tan broken up by lighter bands caused by the straps of your sandals. A sheet of letterhead, garbage, brushes between your legs before blowing onwards. The cries of a child are emergency sirens. And then it happens, you remember.

Remembering causes disgust, especially when an avalanche of images forces you back into reality. You do not live among palm trees, but you'd love to have sand in your garden. You know soon that time will once again be dictated by something far less significant than the transit of the sun. Everything you now have before your eyes will soon disappear through the back window of a taxi. For a month you've been living the original dream of humanity, the dream of independence, where reality only vaguely resembles an alternative lifestyle.

Remember, it's only a holiday; you'll have to leave even if you want to stay. There it is again.

Then you mumble an insulting reply that's jumbled with the dull response of the phone's annoying owner. The reply isn't important; *diga, salam, yes* or *aló*, the accent is irrelevant. Whether you are near or far, you're back.

This time, what started the acid reflux was finding the return trip section of a plane ticket that remarkably was made out in my name. I had landed in Johannesburg because it was the cheapest starting point to terra incognita, and a series of coincidences had left me facing Martin, a Swiss with Bob Marley's dreadlocks. Martin had just crossed Africa in an old ramshackle safari-brown Land Rover, a classic, and was looking for people willing to share some dollars and the cost of petrol. I needed to surprise myself.

It was the end of July and I had fled to the south of Africa for six weeks, taking advantage of a month's holiday and an extra fortnight by way of a mental health issue. My brain no longer worked well. It was serious, but not quite enough to require being put on a psychiatrist's wait list. I had merely started questioning the meaning of the inevitable.

You *have to* work; you *must* take the bus every morning at the same time. Or drive in the same direction, in the same traffic jam, listening to the same radio station with an expression on your face like something out of a wax museum. You *have to* pay the electrical bill, the telephone, the utilities, the children's school, the damn mortgage or the rent. You *have to* go to the office at sunrise and leave at sunset. This is normal; this is what life *is* all about.

Billboards on the street and ads on television proclaimed that the only alternative was to drink Coca-Cola. Then your world would become a factory which would radiate happiness into outer space. The guys from Atlanta had already begun their campaign of replacing the cocaine in the original formula with lysergic acid.

Yes, I too worked in the wonderful world of advertising. I came up with ads, developed ideas that helped you choose the *best* beer, the car *best* suited to your needs, the hotel with the *best* services. I liked that tension, that continuous challenge of ingenuity versus deadlines. I could have devoted myself to writing poetry, but this paid better.

In my defence, I admit that I never did exactly what I was asked to do. You should tell stories concisely, but I always wrote too much. "Yes, very nice, but get rid of half the words." As if writing were like stacking stones.

I used rare expressions, metaphors with a unique foreign cadence and occasionally put forward some original proposals. Lately I was determined to find a way of slipping a street protest into an advertising campaign. Kamikaze tomatoes committed suicide against the ground to avoid falling back into the arms of a head of lettuce; a squatter covered in piercings sold mortgages for a respectable bank; satanic phrases hidden in the texts advertised a gin in green bottles. It was undoubtedly my subconscious sending messages to the other side. Something was wrong.

The year 1999 was strange, different from all the years that had preceded it. There were still a few months to the end of the millennium according to Pope Gregory XIII's mathematicians, who had baptised our calendar for four centuries. The simple numerical occurrence that takes place every thousand years had somehow changed the mood on the street.

The world had divided into two camps: those who were in favour and those who were against the transcendence of dates ending with so many round numbers. The most common reaction was sarcasm and affected curiosity. But there was also a slight feeling of dread. Indifference was inconceivable. People argued in bank line-ups, at the supermarket and in elevators. Each building had a Nostradamus as a porter. Everybody had to have an opinion; raise the thermostat, talk about God and the Antichrist, even though nobody believed anything exceptional was about to happen. Wars would not stop for a day. God would not be descending to Earth to turn us into human beings. It was impossible to think we'd all win the lottery.

In the media, few prophets, clairvoyants or tarot card readers predicted the end of the world. No serious newspaper wasted ink printing catastrophic headlines. It was not profitable. The message, *"you see, I was right, the world did end"* just wasn't on.

The only ones that seemed worried were governments and corporations. They feared that all computers would revert back to some analogue prehistory and stop working as year 99 became 00. Nothing. Can you imagine? In their nightmares, all debts, all transactions, all the wealth and well-being achieved through years of accumulation, gone in a historic second. Abracadabra, now we're all equal again.

It was humanity's second most common dream, the dream of equality.

The last thing I needed during that holiday was to associate with another fugitive. When all was said and done, Martin and his dreads made a reasonably sane ensemble: almost thirty years old, wanting to do things, full beard and various harmless extravagances, fitting for someone who had just crossed Africa in an old 4x4 held together with baling wire. For example, he had invented a language based on sounds which could only be translated into sensations, doubt, joy, confidence, a problem: *"Curucu-cucoo! Pundaee! Cuac-cuac-cuac..."* It was an Esperanto for travellers in foreign lands.

His system was very simple: he first tried speaking in one language and if he was not understood, he tried another. The third time he would invent it. Seconds later he had set up a relationship based on laughter and the fearless acceptance of ridicule. If they don't understand your words, let them understand your emotions. It was a resounding success.

"Sometimes they bet amongst themselves regarding my madness. I could see it in their eyes. You know, nobody attacks crazy people, especially if they're happy. Laughing lunatics are harmless."

There were the two of us in Johannesburg, but we needed a third road trip partner to help defray costs, and this was a problem. Almost everyone who slept at the hostel travelled with a companion. Few people vacation alone, and fewer still have the liberty of forgetting that golden chain called *plans*. Among that small percentage, even fewer were not dangerously insane.

"Inga, her name is Inga, and she speaks little English," this is how Martin introduced her while unfolding a large worn and taped-up Michelin map on the ground. Folded up it was as thick as a Bible. "Should we go to Harare?"

Inga was typically German, neither beautiful nor ugly, fat nor thin. She had brown hair and worked as a nurse in some small Baltic town eleven months of the year. It was always cold there. She knew how to give intramuscular and intravenous injections, how to take a pulse on the carotid artery, and how to change the diapers of ancient grandfathers who would sometimes reach out and caress one of her Teutonic breasts. Inga was the opinion poll model German: self-sufficient, with some higher education, trusting, beer-drinking, with only a sporadic smile, like all the good productive citizens of Northern Europe. It had taken her years to abandon those crazy summers in coastal Spain and fly by herself to Africa. Well, to South Africa, the most developed country on the continent.

Our opinion of her changed when we discovered that she suffered from anxiety attacks every time she thought about the adventure she was on. Instead of getting excited, she became frightened: *"I am alone in Africa, on an unknown route, increasingly far from the airport, from my embassy; from the hospital recommended by my health insurance provider... das is zum kotzen!"* The anxiety attacks could occur while catching a glimpse of baboons running like dogs by the side of the road, or while interacting with a group of peaceful and humble black housewives, or during a routine police road check. The latter was particularly dangerous. Her nervousness made us all suspects in everything: white subversives out to undermine a black government, illegal immigration, and even drug trafficking. Thinking of prison only worsened her anxiety.

Because of this, she began scratching her hands, wrists, and forearms. Insecurity caused her to itch. Within fifteen minutes the first scratches appeared. Within the hour she had started to bleed from small wounds that never healed. Only then would she forget she was in Africa, pull out a first aid kit and patch herself up.

Inga stayed behind at Victoria Falls. Her departure was the closest thing to a primary school sticker swap: "I'll trade you a weird German for a quiet Japanese." Takayuki was small, silent, and also travelled alone. His goal was to cross Africa on a push scooter, which was enough of an excuse for his best friends to vacation elsewhere. He wore clown's shoes that were four sizes too large to push himself along more efficiently and (this was almost a miracle) he had still not been run over by a truck. It was all just a matter of time. Every trucker eventually gets his minute of fame in the yellow press.

In those few African weeks, many extraordinary things happened to this office clerk: I dug up whalebones along empty beaches, climbed huge sand dunes in the desert, learned how to walk unarmed amid lions and elephants, and watched the rising green bubbles of the Zambezi River rapids from below. Almost every day I walked along trails scratched into the jungle or on soft, sandy paths. It was my personal return to a simpler life; a life of innocence, when we still believed we were all free.

Three weeks and many kilometres later, at Windhoek, Namibia, I put my hand in the wrong pocket and pulled out a folded paper; the airline ticket, the return flight. I remembered that I had to go back; this was not my real life. This was just a borrowed life, a holiday.

★

I returned to the animal kingdom of Barcelona sandwiched between a woman with nostalgic eyes and a water filter sales agent who spoke compulsively. He had just finished a week of isolation in a country where he didn't understand a word of their language. I was his ear, the dummy on which he practised his stories about his satisfaction with the buffet at the Sun City Hotel-Casino and his safari amid the black prostitutes of Johannesburg. "That's really dangerous," he repeated, "not like those gay safaris in armoured cars to see wild animals." He practised his best phrases on me, the most striking, which he would later use on his friends and customers. He talked too much.

When the movie started I put on my headphones and turned the volume to zero, determined to confront what was tormenting me: my return to real life, not too dissimilar to the life of the water filter salesman.

I took out the wrinkled piece of paper I had left in my pocket since Harare and read it again: *'Life is everything that happens while you're making other plans.'* That phrase was from a certain loud-mouthed character named John Lennon who was shot and killed one cold December night. Lower the curtain, the show's over. I had a room papered with maps, books and magazines that took me to the end of the world without leaving home. I wanted to go to all these paradises, but 'one of these days' or 'in a few years' had become my favourite excuses to avoid the commitment that involves betting on what you really want to do in life.

When I opened the door of my mortgaged apartment I knew that I had to go. On the other side was the life of a stranger with steady work, routines, obligations and television. Staying meant taking the path to security, and that meant planning a nice funeral. I had already buried a previous life I was supposed to live. Why not do it again? Why not kill the life you're supposed to live?

Why not start again?

Eight years had passed since that first great adventure, when I had landed in Madrid on an Aeroflot plane with stops in Recife, Isla de Sal,

Algiers and Moscow; half the world. Now life was again beginning to become predictable. Why not change history?

That night, after having sniffed each other for two hours and talking about the month and a half of living separately, I confessed to Anna that I had not brought her back anything from Africa. Yes, I was a miserable cretin who could only offer her candy-coated words, wrapped in sweet poison.

"Would you like to drive around the world with me?"

Who hasn't dreamt at least once of travelling around the world?

To put it another way, who hasn't at some point wanted to start a new life closer to their dreams and farther from reality?

Seated at my side, Anna is still sceptical. After nine months of building castles in the sky, she's not sure this is the way. She turns her head, looks at me and smiles with pursed lips. This is perhaps just another dream from which we'll awake at any moment to find ourselves entrapped in a new series of sticky routines.

Pinch me, please.

Thirty-six hours before our planned date of departure, Anna received the results of a medical test that assured her an operation was needed. Some cells from her cervix disagreed with our plans and conspired to fill our heads with disastrous messages. *Nothing is as good as it seems. The trip is a bad idea. Everything can go wrong.* That was a month ago, when at the last minute we delayed the trip, "just as we were about to leave." A terrifying phrase if it ends there.

But no, Anna pinches me. It hurts.

She cranes her neck with evil satisfaction to look at the intense blue sky through the windscreen. She must detect the hordes of odours filing past as the city undresses itself of cement at sixty kilometres an hour: carbon monoxide, sewers, air fresheners, cheap perfume, fried food, freshly baked bread, hot asphalt. The same smells that fatten with the heat of summer. We know we're leaving, but our bodies continue entwined with the logic of driving along a known path. There are still the same buildings, the same bridges, the same traffic lights, and the same music on the radio. *"And now, once again for your listening pleasure, this summer's top song...!"*

We're still at home. Nothing has changed on this bright June day. In fact, we're only going to Ikea to buy a new shelf to arrange our lives better at The Independent Republic of My House. We move away for a beer at a different beach. We go to the supermarket to fill up the fridge because it's the beginning of another month. *Have you brought the Visa card?* The left side of my brain senses something new in the chain of events and grabs the steering wheel harder.

Pinch me again.

In the rear-view mirror, the number of cars following us to the east multiplies, as if escape were a shared dream. As if we all had chosen the path of uncertainty. But no, little by little they disappear; they pass us or find their own way. Our new home, a 1991 Mitsubishi L300/Delica 4x4 has the same aura as the Volkswagen hippy-vans of the 70s. It's another slow nuisance bloated with luggage.

Inhale. I fill my lungs to slough off another layer of old skin. I'm still not sure that this is real and not another invented story, not another weekend stamped with an expiration date.

Exhale. On the sides of the road the wind is blowing. Oaks, pines and maples shake their manes like stressed out backup dancers.

Inhale. The clouds rush by and birds let themselves be dragged from one tree to another like they are on some wild roller coaster ride. A young man on the road remains perplexed.

Exhale. Every day that ends brings us one step closer to death. What should we do? Sit and wait for it? I prefer to run, run towards it.

Inhale. I feel my pocket but can't find my telephone or my anchor of keys that weighed me down so much. My instinctive anxiety returns, I'm drowning. The telephone, where is my telephone?

A gust of wind blasts through the window and decontaminates the van. Some scales fly out, others cling desperately to the skin. The odour of narrow roads violently hits our faces: the essence of forest, fresh grass and humidity, the smell of recently-cut wood, of thick wood smoke, concentrated stench of...

"Cow shit... Anna! We have left the city!"

The aroma appears and disappears capriciously. Every time it returns it reminds us that the rest of our lives, what happens after this and what we don't know is going to happen, is starting. My skin erupts in millions of small volcanoes, I *feel* it. The whole body and every latent bacterium, every molecule of flesh, blood, fat, fingernail and bone reverberates frantically with a new anxiety. We're on the road.

"Do you realize that? This is what freedom is like outside the big cities of Europe; smelling cow shit every day!"

Innocently, we have decided to drive around the world. The reality is we have set out to overland across some of the worst terrain on the planet. We have changed our large apartment for a micro living-space of just five square metres, and a secure job for an insecure but more intense life. You can only regret what you didn't do, never what you tried but failed at, even if this ends up being the worst of our failures.

"Go around the world? How? With what money? Towards where? What did you hit your head against?" I remember the confused look on Anna's face as if she were in front of me.

"Why not? We share our savings, we rent out the apartment to pay off the mortgage, we buy a used 4x4 in good shape so we can live inside, and we find work along the way to earn some money. Yes, it's madness, but it's madness for the unusual, not for the impossible."

Within half an hour she said yes. By then I had already told her about my discoveries in front of a large map. It's possible to drive through the south of Europe to the Middle East, and descend into Africa to Cape Town, where all roads finish. Afterwards we'll see, but we could cross the Atlantic by boat to South America, like my grandparents did. We could start again in Tierra del Fuego, reach the furthest point north of Alaska, and return back to Barcelona by way of the Siberia-Finisterre highway.

That highway does not exist, but I didn't tell her that.

Nine months later the smell of pre-Pyrenean cow dung acts like an elixir, Channel No. 5 for my guts. Every time I inhale I remember that it's not another day. It's today, at this moment, right now. Exhale; relief and uneasiness shift to shake my foundations. The dreams of so many centuries of work and routine are here, beyond the barn and the fertilised fields glimpsed through the trees, all within the blink of an eye. History is not written in stone.

Anna continues smiling.

We first met at her office, in the late afternoon. She was tired and I tried to do my good deed for the day by speaking nonsense. My Good Samaritan act vanished quickly when I noticed the contrast between her 1.8-metre-tall Amazon body and her make-up free face. No war paint here. *It is what it is, kid.* Over her nose, two pieces of sky laughed on my account.

What a match.

We started having dinner, walking on the beach and making love a couple times a week. We progressed from sharing our immediate desires to sharing those things you only tell your pillow: things which come out when you're drunk or very excited. The sense of feminine practicality was in her blood and won out from the very beginning: "things are the way they are, there is what there is and what there isn't, there isn't, at least not yet. We shall see if it happens. Who knows?" Her philosophy was to live one day at a time. Enjoy the daily routine of the city, the same which awaited me after work.

What could possibly be better than having coffee, beer or rum with the same old friends in the pub at the corner?

In the city, you can choose between God and the Devil. You can go to the theatre or the cinema, go to a dance, tally up planes in the sky or hug your family like a real Italian. You can have a bubble bath and spend the weekend in the mountains or in a shopping mall. In fact, you can do anything. Cities are anonymous; you can only see what you are allowed to see.

A face. The front of a house. An illustrious last name. Music at full blast, clothes. In the city it's easy to disappear and stop being the honest family man to become Lord of whatever you want: leather straps, dog collars, and harnesses anatomically designed for human jaws. That bruise came from when you fell. That scratch came from your cat. The vacation money was stolen right at the front door of the bank. The car too. You would never bet it at a poker table. You can tramp around neighbourhoods where honourable housewives would never be seen shopping. You hang yourself and resuscitate every morning, forget your documents and use pseudonyms, artistic names, Lolita or Gabriel; complete angels. You can check out dives where you would not expect to meet up with your children, or your parents.

In the city you can be a social devil: friendly, kind, charitable, honourable. While you choose all the available adjectives, you can live the life of the famous or the phony, run after balls of different sizes and cover it up with the routine of a stable job. When you get bored, you can sink yourself into the Internet or surf channels until you find some surreal TV show from Korea. No, urban life is not all bad.

Ours orbited around the same old stops. *The Everyday Bus Company announces the departure of your regular bus number 12,330. From home to work, from work to home, with stops at the goddamn bathroom mirror, the bastard's desk, the underhanded hand of your office companion, the Deception Bar, the wink from the mannequin in the window, the 'here we go again' exhaustion, and finally, with any luck, two sincere words from the eyes of a friend: "you alright?"*

"Tired. But we must go on, right?"

That's how it went until The Click. It really was a click, the trigger that set off a pickpocket right in the heart of Barcelona. The unique click sound of Anna's purse emerging amidst thousands of clicks and repetitive sounds. The click that decided the future by sending an alarm signal to the brain which calculated instinctively: we must defend ourselves without getting knifed in the liver. The PAF! as Anna reacted, slapped the face of the pickpocket and kicked him between the legs. It surprised us all. The poor fellow folded over and started to shrink. She said something along the lines of "get out of here, and don't be such an asshole". I was beside myself.

Let's start again. Hello Anna, we met five months ago, but it appears I still don't know you. Who are you?

Forty-eight hours later we descended a ravine in the Pyrenees with some friends. We travelled along the river and rappelled with ropes between waterfalls. We jumped between pools of transparent and frigid water while splashing about lazily. This was paradise. Then we came upon a 12-metre-high cliff that dropped off into a deep pool that came directly from the Arctic.

"I bet you won't jump," I boldly stated.

"How about you? Would you jump?" she replied challengingly.

"Certainly, but you first."

Anna jumped. I was doomed.

Now, while the smell of cow dung conquers the universe, we again jump. As hopeless optimists, we believe we know what will happen: a man and a woman move into a house on wheels. They live many adventures, they are happy and four years later they return to their starting point. It seems simple.

The Everyday Bus Company announces the departure of unique voyage number one, destination the end of the world.

All we know about Africa is that there are wars, hunger, and vast empty spaces on maps. The roads are good, bad, or non-existent. There are policemen collecting souvenirs and black men in loincloths and Armani suits. There are palm trees and elephants. There are stories of foreigners disappearing forever, swallowed up by the land of Tarzan, that illegal migrant who became king of the jungle. And there are tribes, deserts, malaria, the Nile, weapons, pyramids, and some Muslim fanatics. We know we're going to be robbed. We know that more than once we'll end up losing.

I look at Anna. I try to imagine her reaction when we face a dangerous situation. Will she have so much courage in Africa?

I outstretch my arm blindly, caress her cheek, and put my finger in her eye.

"Get out!"

"Do you realize we've left?"

"Yes," she replies while sticking her head out the window to feel the wind. The same revolutionary air pulls the last sticky spots of

Barcelona off our skin. In front of the windscreen there is an intense blue sky criss-crossed with green and brown rays. "I will believe we've really left when returning becomes harder than continuing."

★

The world changes through the windscreen. It's not a cataclysm, nor that mystic illumination that raises you to the edge of good karma. It's the distance; kilometres enrich the soul.

These are the opening moments, the originals, the certain and emotional succession of first times. It doesn't matter if you don't understand too well where you are. During the first sunset in an unfamiliar place you look for a remote dark corner. At the first dawn you get your first backache after sleeping for the first time on a mattress that's three miserable centimetres thick. At the first truck stop the first discord arrives and the first dubious looks follow us. In the second road bar, we hear the first gurgled words in a different language. Outside, the first honking horn becomes distant, like the first pages of a virgin book.

I raise my arm to return the first wave from another van and remember that it's been two days since I last showered. Perhaps I should lower my arm.

The Pyrenees Mountains continue to give way to surly peaks and a mosaic of French fields, fenced, ordered and squeezed to the last square metre, repeating themselves on each side of the highway. The landscape in front of us is the same as the landscape behind us; the only thing that changes is the shape of the white houses or the green and yellowish tone of the crops. On the horizon another ancient and walled village rises, with the church steeple towering over the red tiled roofs. The road signs mark detours, parking lots, service stations and even the distance to the next toilet. All that is left to chance is schizophrenia, unexplained murders, monsters lurking in innocent looking villages, passion or accidents caused by parties that ended too late. Europe seems like an organised country where every square of the map has a supervisor who hates surprises.

The skyline changes its profile and becomes more remote, a pointless but effective pursuit. Every day we must undo the daily trace of the sun. May the next dawn awaken us earlier until the hours confuse themselves and the strings of time become entangled. We take some unnecessary detours: narrow paths that end at the edge of cultivated or wild river shores, anonymous old villages, new vistas that always look towards the east.

On the fifth day, after the first curves of the Alps, a great STOP sign appears. It is so large and exaggerated there is no possibility it would ever go unnoticed. A Swiss police officer automatically lifts his arm in a clean, academic gesture. No doubt he received an Honours Degree at the Swiss Border Guard University.

"Bonjour"

"Bonjour"

"What are you carrying there?"

The policeman looks at us with curiosity. I suppose we display the idiotic smiles of those who finally start to walk the path they have dreamt about for far too long. Behind us lies the future: canned food, containers full of drinking water, old tools and the chaos of uncertainty. In the same pocket I have an incomplete list, five wrinkled sheets of paper, which the policeman takes suspiciously between two fingers. He fears he may be holding the bacteriologically contaminated object that will end all life on planet Earth.

Apart from Spanish there is something else he doesn't understand and his nostrils flare instinctively. His eyes move from one side to the other, peeking at the interior of the van over my shoulder. "What is this?" he asks opening the papers. This is too hippie for him. He looks at our foreign faces, and licks his parted lips in a straight line. He retreats into the passports, Spanish from Barcelona, Spanish from Buenos Aires. He looks again at the general disorder, and shrugs his shoulders in resignation. We are white; the only strange thing is our happiness.

"Perhaps it would be better if we say that we're only carrying our home," suggests Anna.

And it's true, because behind us is our bedroom with a skylight window in the ceiling, a living room with shelves full of more or less useful items and a small library behind the co-pilot's seat. There's a kitchen with a frying pan, pot and cutlery as well as a 2.5-kilogram butane-gas cylinder, and a collection of tools in a drawer. That's the workshop. All of this in the same five square metres. Over the ceiling there's an attic filled with things you usually save just in case. The bathroom is as large as the fields and the view out the windows changes almost every day. They even have curtains.

'Home is where you find it' proclaimed a famous Smirnoff advertisement at the beginning of the 90's. I turn my head and can't avoid distorting my idiotic smile: this has nothing to do with the illustrated encyclopaedic definition. Our home is a house of gypsies, an old van returning to the Maghreb from anywhere in Europe, a refuge for vagabonds, a nomadic and lonely caravan parked under the street lamp of some anonymous alley.

Now we're foreigners everywhere we go.

Switzerland is like France but with fewer road signs. Everything is immaculate, orderly and clean, though the streets of Geneva reek of dead cat: buildings collect all their organic waste under the stairs in sparkling containers picked up by the city trucks once a week. It's a true natural resource.

We pass by a house surrounded by dozens of stiff garden gnomes with the same idiotic smile I see in the mirror: they look like ten marijuana smokers locked up in a small bathroom. It all makes sense in this fable of a town surrounded by vertiginous mountains covered in trees and white hats. I bet Snow White will be around the next corner holding up the hem of her gown.

But no, what I see is a stable with an advertisement on its roof for 'Fromagerie Le Solliat', a cheese factory. The place is idyllic, perfect, a postcard printed on super fine Swiss paper, impeccable. Some twenty rustic houses built of stone and wood on both sides of the *rue du Village*, the village's street, the only street. Next to the open doors of a carpenter's workshop are pots filled with flowers and tools. Behind that are some fat cows penned up in a corral. Beyond there is forest.

Next to the barn owned by Heidi's grandfather lies the old *camperized* Land Rover I met in Africa. I look through the dirty windows; the open scars in the seats display a flesh of foam. The drawers are disjointed bones filled with dust, tired, the belly of a buffalo tortured by bad roads. Every scratch opens up a mental photo album and all from only forty days that I travelled with it.

"Martin?" I ask a man holding a hammer on a cushion of sawdust.

"Go up. Second floor, on your right. The door's open. If he's not there, he will be at the bar. In the village. Down below." He answers in spurts before putting two nails in his mouth.

The door is indeed open, but there's nobody home. When we descend, the carpenter raises his thumb towards the back of the house while he continues sucking his nails. In Switzerland nails come in three flavours, Roast Lamb, Emmental Cheese, and Abbey Beer.

Martin came back from Africa a bit over a month ago and it appears he has returned into the rhythm of his old life. He left his windsurfing board in the nursery by the lake and found a job in a small company which produces a line of erotic watches for Arab sheikhs and eccentric millionaires. He is not sorry to be back.

"*Putain,* where the hell are you going with all this stuff?" was the first thing he said on seeing the van.

He's right. The stuff on the roof looks like a bump on the head. When you live in the excess of cities it's difficult to distinguish between the essential and the accessory. You've decided to leave, but what are you prepared to sacrifice? You pack too many clothes, too many precautions, too many prejudices and too many useless items.

"What is this?" asks Martin, on seeing a square box plastered with pictures of the most obedient girl in the world.

"Her name is Maggie. She's an inflatable doll. It was a gift from a friend so we'd always have someone to talk to when we became bored with talking to each other. She's the best. If you squeeze her left nipple she says *"Oh yes! Oh yes!"* She always agrees with you.

He looks at me disconcertedly.

The table in his house is topped with bread, cheese, wine and some recent stains. He has recovered the life he had stored in boxes before leaving for his overland trip, but he still has his Leatherman knife and many other things on hand, like the drum with tribal inscriptions from Zambia. Sometimes he still blurts out a selection of some of his most absurd expressions, like the *"curucucu!"* he lets out when he's happy. He doesn't have a television set and doesn't read the papers. He simply went back to a quiet life next to the lake, surrounded by old friends.

The theme of our conversation is travel; routes from the past and adventure plans for the future. About the rented Mongolian horse that tossed his rider, who ran after it through the forest towards the corral they had left five hours before. About the suspicions of the Sudanese police and the forbidden pictures of the Dalai Lama that entered illegally into Tibet. About the sad joy of Havana, the risks involved with Mexican mescal, and the mountains of Peru. About Japanese tourists who reach the end of the world without speaking any language other than Japanese, and of travellers who no longer recognise their homes.

But the story that takes us the furthest is that of Yak, a Swiss who wanted to reach Tibet by bicycle. The two years of the trip became four, then five, and now six. When he stopped in front of the Potala Palace he asked himself what he would do if he returned home. So he decided to keep going. He disembarked in Japan with hardly any money and found a job in a hotel cleaning rooms, pushing a cart piled with sheets and scraping off small condoms that were stuck to the floor. He crossed the Pacific and reached Alaska and from there pedalled all the way to Patagonia. In the United States he was poor because he only owned a bicycle. In Guatemala he was rich because he owned a bicycle. He crossed the Atlantic to South Africa and we met up with him in Zimbabwe. He was pedalling his way north, back to his home, wherever that might be.

We enter Italy through the Great St. Bernard Pass. We splash about in an inundated Venice and we descend down the Italian Adriatic Coast. We avoid Rome so we won't fall into the chaos of August, but we end up trapped by the noisy tourism of Rimini. We cross the Abruzzo Range towards the south and for two hours we try to enter Naples. We follow the road signs but once and again we return to the same crossroad, the same plaza in the same village far from the city. It's impossible, 100 kilometres ago we were on that exact corner. The fellow who installed the road signs had a twisted sense of humour.

When we eventually arrive in the centre of Naples it's 11 p.m. and the party is out of control. Thousands and thousands of excited people, move, drink and yell at the same time. It's almost surreal, the closest thing to being at the last carnival during the end of the world. At midnight the bells strike and Dolce & Gabanna turn into Sodom & Gomorra.

A comet inexorably approaches the city. It's all now, everything must be now.

The streets are full, swarming, packed and overflowing with some of the most extreme type of human being; a kind of biological entity whose genes die out if it tries to reproduce outside of its familiar chaotic ecosystem. It's an explosion of hormones destined to conquer the world by way of hugs, pizza, and opera singers: the Southern Italians.

Mamma mia.

Street festivals in Naples are over the top, a modern bacchanalia in the epicentre of Camorra country, the mother of all Italian mafias. Everything is allowed. Nobody has bothered to close off the centre of the city and cars mix with people in waves. Emotional tsunamis clean the chassis of our van with the latest Versace designs. Two girls jump on the roof of a parked car looking for something while oscillating to the rhythm of the music coming from a nearby bar. Vespas with three or four passengers on board come from every direction, without any sense of order. Two men communicate by way of shouts with half their bodies sticking out the window of their cars. *Vedi Napoli e poi muori* prophesies graffiti on the side of a building. It's fantastic.

In the centre of this apparent disorder, a team of workers takes up the cobbling on a street. Nobody cares if they work for city hall or if they're digging a tunnel to rob a bank. Today, anything goes, it's the Festival of the Madonna Del Carmine, the Virgin of Carmen, and God is partying.

Prostitutes brighten the corners with fires burning in steel barrels to further heat up the summer night. A neon light in a store claims *La notte a Napoli é bella.* The third version in two days of the bolero 'Solamente Una Vez', this time with maracas, emanates from an old bar. A bottle is smashed against a wall. The street's fruit market is open, empty, but open. We slowly move through the laughter and whispers of sellers who, five metres from a deaf and mute policeman, keep asking "hashish, telephone, camera, hashish, what are you looking for my friend?" On the stage built in the plaza there is a band playing African music. Welcome to Naples! Long live anarchy!

In front of an alley we spot the rusty remains of an old Fiat 128 painted in blue and white. It's an historical monument covered in square letters: DIEGO, FORZA NAPOLI, MARADONA.

Naples is real, poor, scandalous, and yes, Maradonian. The rebel hero, cursed by the owners of soccer's international federations, led a revolt in 1987 to resurrect the word "pride." The agricultural south had always lost the annual football wars against the industrialised north. That is, until that magical year, one thousand nine hundred and eighty-seven, when Diego Maradona became the stamp of a saint, the symbol of hope, the spiritual Godfather of the south of Italy. The Napoli, a medium almost-small team, won the Scudetto for the first time in its history and then went on to win the European Cup. History is not written in stone.

"*Bongiorno.* Where can *io* leave the *furgona*? Where can *io trovare* a safe place for the *macchina*?" I ask nervously, in a jumble of languages, to a couple of policemen who are admiring the human spectacle.

"A safe place, in Naples? Bwah-ha-ha-ha-ha!" they burst out in gales of laughter. I laugh with them, naturally, what are you going to do? Ha-ha-ha...

And now, where are we going?

All the entrances to parking lots are lower than the van. In other words, there are no parking spots for us. A small voice, half angelic, half demonic, recommends against parking on just any street, much less during the nocturnal manifestations of partying Southern Italians. For the first time I noticed the vast illuminated silhouette of Mount Vesuvius, the symmetrical and dark sleeping giant that crouches behind the city.

Sleeping in the dormant volcano might be the safest option tonight.

★

"*Spagnoli!* I was with the Navy in Spain. Giovanni, do you remember those Spaniards that we fought in Madrid?" asks an old man to his buddy, enthusiastically recalling the memories of a life that might not have been his.

"What?" asks the doubting grandfather of all grandfathers, stretching out his ancient turtle-like neck. He lacks hearing aids, he lacks teeth, but has a wealth of years.

"Of course you remember those Spaniards we beat up in Madrid" he repeats raising his wrinkled fists in Torre Anunziatta, several kilometres south of Naples, deep in the heart of Italy. We are looking for a beach and a public shower.

When they finish telling us their war stories, *there was four of them and we were three, Puerta del Sol, Franco, Mussolini, women, but they were hot,* they send us to Lido Panzarotto, a great cement parking lot enclosed by grey crumbling walls, connected to the beach by a small door. Next to it is a beverage stand held up by yellow metal panels and three men scattered among a jumble of chairs and tables. In one corner is a mountain of fishing nets and on the other side there is an old abandoned car. It is a decadent fortress isolated from the sea.

"Buonassera" I say as a greeting.

"Buona sera" replies the trio.

"Would it be alright if I *parcare* here and *dormire la notte*?" I ask, reinventing the Italian language.

"Certainly. No problem. It's quite alright," reply Nello, Andrea and Franco in turn, 150 years between the three of them, while they offer us a couple of chairs.

Before sitting down we look out through the door that leads to the beach. On the other side, some two hundred metres away extend the ruins of a fortified island.

"Look, black sand," says Anna.

"Of course, from Vesuvius, it's a volcanic area."

"And tomatoes, onions…"

On the sand and over the waves floats a giant red and white salad. The entire beach, as far as the eye can see, is planted with thousands of salty and gleaming tomatoes and onions, ready for harvesting. An ocean that brings fresh vegetables!

"It's the Lido Panzarotto!" says Franco, accentuating the vowels. "Every evening after five the tomatoes from the canning factory come in with the tide. The onions start to arrive at seven. Every morning at sunrise, children clean up the beach, and then the crowds arrive."

Nature is like that.

We set up our kitchen, the antique pot which belonged to Anna's grandmother, an assortment of cups and plastic mugs and we start boiling some water to make coffee.

"That's a pot for pasta. It's going to make Enrico hungry!" says Nello pointing to his brother, who saunters up walking behind his stomach.

"No, this is our pot for everything, pasta, coffee, soup…"

"You're going to cook pasta?" asks Enrico.

"No, it's for coffee."

"Coffee? In that pot? Coffee is taken short, *ristretto!*"

"Who's going to cook pasta?" asks his mother, a strong and restless grandmother, who sits next to the fishing nets.

Nello is a 40-year-old mechanic, and a decade ago emigrated with his wife and children to work at a Mercedes Benz factory in Germany. Every summer he comes back to Torre Anunziatta to enjoy his months' vacation with his family. When it's time to go back, he phones the company and says he is too ill to return.

"*Molto malato!* Stress, I ate a poisoned fish. I have an enlarged stomach, my feet are deformed, I can't even walk! Two months!" he repeats lifting his fingers in a sign of victory. Family is family.

His healing therapy consists of fishing every night with Enrico, who permanently resides by the sea. They float out over the Mediterranean in a small boat, drop their nets in front of the beach, and collect them before sunrise. They pull between 50 and 100 kilos of fresh fish daily. Some they sell to restaurants in the city, some are left over for their mother who prepares snacks at the bar on the beach.

Andrea approaches the pile of nets and begins to extend them with care. They have to fix the strands that broke last week. They all get together and while new knots replace holes, they talk. In Italy, silence is not an option.

"Andrea scuba-dives to depths of 10 to 15 metres in his search for octopus."

"La *mamma* had ten sons and now has fifty-four grandchildren."

"Pompeii is an incredible place with statues of people who died two thousand years ago."

"You have to be careful with motorcyclists, they're the ones that will steal from you. They're protected by the Camorra."

"The beach, the coast of Sorrento, that's what's important... the coast is beautiful!"

★

The next night, after dining on crusty bread with onion and hot peppers, with pate, with several cooked plates and beers which appear from a refrigerator hidden behind the counter, after several stories of mainland animals, of fish with four eyes and octopuses that fed a family or fed on a family, Nello invites me to set out the nets on his boat. He only invites me: in southern Italy a woman's place is at home.

Anna bites her tongue, enough to make it bleed, and enough to make her seek refuge in the van and cure herself with chocolate. I heard on the radio that the dream of 90% of Italian women is to go on holiday without their husbands.

Ten minutes later we push the boat into the water. It's a moonless night and the darkness, an inky blackness printed on a black background, slowly devours us. Nello guides the boat diagonally across the waves that are trying to overturn us. They intensify and push us with greater force towards the shore. The sea knows the boat will scratch its womb and stir its body.

I position myself at the bow, far from the taca-taca-taca of the motor that sounds like a chef's knife on a cutting board. I'm the umbrella, the sponge that absorbs the salty foam that breaks against the wooden bow.

When the motor slows, Enrico, strong and fat, begins to row. Then the waves surrender and Nello lays out the nets, metre by metre. He is careful to ensure the floats don't become entangled with the weights, and the grey rhomboids descend gently. Afterwards he points the boat towards the small fortified island, illuminated by the reflections of the lights from shore. It's been some time since the Saracen tower was abandoned, and every year it falls apart a bit more, like a sand castle surrounded by old scattered Lego blocks. They didn't mention we were going there, and my imagination races.

"On this island they used to torture people, hang them, guillotine them," explains Enrico passing his finger across his neck.

If I turned my back on them they might harpoon me and throw my body into the water until I disappear. Or even better, they might chop me up into little pieces so that Mamma can cook me. Tomorrow I'll be the daily special on the menu. And Anna is on the beach...

I hardly know them. Our lives crossed some 30 hours ago, we played the role of visitors and I know little about the locals. I only know what they are willing to say and what I'm able to understand. Neapolitan fishermen, a beach with a salad, a huge family, they're all friends, running a bar in summer, builder and mechanic the rest of the year. We understand each other through our eyes, our body language and some macaroni Italian. And then there's *mamma* and things which

I remember from when I was a child in another city thousands of kilometres away. Surprising, they're much the same as here.

But travelling means trusting; to let yourself be taken by strangers to physical or mental places you would never arrive to alone. Trust. Just by allowing others to take the rudder, you can discover places that you didn't even know existed.

My imagination soars, but I'm still soaking wet below this starry sky. I hallucinate about the dark landscape and my absurd fear of becoming shipwrecked this close to home. Trust, trust. In the west, many people distrust anything unfamiliar, or anything that is not habitual. If faces have different features or different skin tones, we must be cautious. If the words they use are different, we must doubt. We have to find what is hidden behind that glance because something is always hidden. And we must be suspicious, in case they do something to harm us. Something – whatever it might be. If they cover themselves too much, they're religious fanatics. If they wear loincloths, they're savages. We must distrust because they're different from us, different from the traditions which we grew up with. It's understood, naturally, *our traditions are the only right ones.*

We arrive at the rocks outlined by the echoes of light and we navigate between the massive boulders. Infidel stones hide rocks that are even older, trapezoidal shaped, put there by Venetians a thousand years ago. Stones inhabited by spirits that cannot die, witnesses of violent betrayals. In front of me I see Enrico's fat finger slicing his neck again. A shiver runs down my spine.

But we must trust. Fear can grip you, but one must learn to appease it, to control it. We must trust. France, Switzerland, Italy and Greece are not that different from Spain. Our destiny lies much further than that, after Turkey, where the footsteps over the tightrope become less certain.

The beach is deserted, and there is nothing distinguishable between the rocks – just shadows which cast monsters and ghosts that flicker with doubt. They're my own private ghosts.

The boat remains silent. The only sound comes from the waves hitting the wooden sides of the hull, and the whispering of fear.

We must trust. Especially when every evening we must find a different place to sleep: the street, the parking lot, next to a church or a gas station, on the beach or between some bushes. Will it be safe here? Are truck drivers sounding their horns to say hello or to tell us to get out of the way? Why can't that man get his eyes off us? Why are those others giving us a furtive look?

Fear is inevitable when you take the first steps toward places where no-one is expecting you. Places where you don't have a reservation.

Fear that they're going to steal from you or that you are going to be assaulted, shot, hit by bullets which were never aimed at you. Fear of disappearing, of disappointment and blood poisoning. Fear of never again having a good job, of contracting malaria, of not being understood, of corrupt policemen filing trumped-up charges against you. Fear of the long knife of a fisherman during an innocent night outing, of religious fanatics, of accidents hiding around the next curve, of crashing into a Coca-Cola truck in some forgotten corner of Africa.

In this world, of all possible deaths, that would be the most absurd.

On a 24th of July we disembark from the car ferry in Patras, Greece. The streets are being repaired, the traffic is skittish and an employee of a gas station, hospitably, threatens to send us to the emergency ward if we do not move the van from where we've parked it. No matter. We'll find another village. Our confidence increases and our fears begin to recede.

When you live on the road, most of your plans are useless. It's the trip that decides what's going to happen. You become conditioned by your body, your van, the roads, by your interactions with others, and by your head. And there's always one part of that equation that doesn't listen to you.

We have already surpassed the first major crisis, the first major fight, when the trip around the world was about to finish at the heel of the Italian boot. It's difficult to find equilibrium between the emotion of open spaces and the emotion of the heart.

"We can't continue like this," said Anna one particularly cloudy afternoon.

"Continue? We've just started..."

"That's why."

Before we left, we knew we'd have problems. It isn't easy to share life 24 hours a day, seven days a week, every month. Love can drive you to murder.

That period of adjustment was part of the new reality. The lack of friends to confide in and the lack of personal spaces lasted a week. The seismic shock left us no alternative but to talk, and to talk about everything. When you're uncomfortable with something, you should say it. Nothing can be of such little importance that it's not worth mentioning. But discussing something is not the same as agreeing with something. That's why we began insulting each other.

It was a natural, spontaneous combustion during a turbulent afternoon. The recriminations increased in tone, neither of us ceded ground, and both of us were right about some stupid difference of opinion. We were still marking our territories like a couple of dogs urinating on new tires.

"Idiot."

"Bastard."

"Imbecile."

"Jerk."

"Hard-headed donkey."

"Gob of spit."

"Mange with legs."

"Two legged cockroach."

"Old urinal."

"Toad diarrhoea."

"Cap de suro."

"Please insult me in some Christian language if it's not too much trouble."

"Cork head! It's Catalan! Four years living in Barcelona and you still don't understand Catalan, you idiot!"

"You think *Cap de suro* is a decent insult? You could exert yourself a bit more... You have nothing worse to say?"

"What do you think of 'genetic malformation'?"

"We're going to cross isolated regions, violent areas, places where people speak languages that we have no dictionary for and situations where all of these things are combined. If we want to survive we have to get along well, mosquito brain."

"I know semen stain. If I didn't love you I would not be able to stand your fascist face."

"Mistake."

"Metre-and-a-half haemorrhoid"

"Entrapped fart."

"Donkey."

"You can't repeat yourself! You lose!"

After that day, every time we had a problem we would insult each other. At first with anger, but when we started to improvise we would forget our differences and laugh. *Accidental result of a bender, ill-fated abortion, damned virus, meat scarecrow.* Our unfettered blood-rage leaves us meek and able to discuss the real problem. *Rat from a Chinese restaurant, tumour, mange with legs, platypus, worm.* It's a form of therapy designed to survive an unexpected reality show: ourselves.

The road that leaves Athens towards the north is bordered by cypresses and some orchards of oranges and lemons. By its side runs a fast stream which the undecided asphalt crosses over and over again. August is a generous month, the month of ripe figs and juicy blackberries hanging on spiny bushes. Outside the cities nothing seems important.

Small clusters of white houses with gardens full of apples are permanently stationed next to the road. Women dressed in black, widows that continue with the age-old tradition of mourning for five years, walk by themselves along the shoulder of life.

My mouth draws a bitter smile while I try to find a place for a new thought. There's a certain strange sensation, hard, uncomfortable, that is pushing to escape to the surface while we drive along in silence. Two days ago we discovered the van open and burglarised, almost empty. They took many items, some useful and many useless. We knew that it would happen one day; we had assimilated it as an unavoidable evil. What we were not prepared for was that it would rob us of our confidence.

We spent a few days in Athens. The scenery was perfect, ancient neighbourhoods with narrow streets, archaeological remains integrated into the architecture of the city, a decadent chaos and the original soul of Western civilisation floating all around us. We didn't know where exactly, but according to the guidebooks, it was here.

Social justice. Redistributing wealth makes sense. I had expected this excuse in preparation for being robbed in Africa. But we're still in Europe, there's still a long way to go.

On either side of the route that follows another white valley, the walls are sprayed with holes equipped with ropes and boards. On the top of a natural stone pillar, 100 metres up, perches one of the orthodox monasteries of Meteora. Yes, we could travel like touristic hermits, like those organised groups that never mix with the locals, that never get lost. People who deposit their faith in a tour designed to confirm what they have seen in a brochure. Tours whose only interests are old rocks, reasonable souvenirs, scenery and pictures.

But no, travelling like a hermit doesn't make sense. I don't believe in the silent contemplation of scenery and historical monuments when the greatest spectacle in the world is the human circus. All you have to do is sit by the window of a cafe and open your eyes. The styles of clothing, the way of driving, of talking and communicating, of touching or avoiding touch changes as home becomes more distant. An enormous quantity of emotion remains entrenched in looks and unconscious gestures.

During Ramadan, many Muslims refuse to greet women during the day. In the United States men and women greet with a rapid squeeze of the hand. Often in Spain, both men and women greet with two kisses; in France with three. In Argentina almost all men greet with a kiss to the cheek, but don't try that in Mexico. Inuit traditionally rub their noses together. In Central and northern South America young people greet each other by slowly tapping their clenched fists together. In Africa, a hand greeting can be fairly long between squeezes, cracking knuckles and wrists. Never raise your thumb at an Iranian, you're telling him to shove it up his ass. They tend not to take this well. *Oops.*

We park in front of a rusty sign next to a monastery. 'WELCOME' it says in English. As we hike towards the wall of the valley I remember Jakob, a German with whiskers that twisted up at the end like a true Prussian Kaiser. Last night at the campground, he showed us how to take apart the door so we could repair the broken lock. Later, he took out a case of Bavarian beer from his camper and gave us a small computer fan *because in Africa it gets really hot.* Before disappearing into his wheeled home, he offered up an extraordinary concert by blowing into a plastic sprinkler. Good medicine to forget Athens.

Living in isolation would be a waste.

The path leads away from the ancient monastery and climbs, keeping in equilibrium along the cliff until it reaches a grilled gate secured with a lock. Fear is a heavy and annoying load, a useless load that keeps you chained with prejudice. On the other side of the gate is a contorted staircase, twisted against the side of the cliff. At the top there must be a cave, and a hermit.

Ancient skulls of orthodox monks at the Megalo Monastery, Meteora, Greece.

Fear is more dangerous than routine.

I prepare the camera to immortalise a moment of minimalist beauty: white rock, decrepit staircase, blue sky, a world devoid of emotions, secure, controlled; the ultra-pasteurised country of a TV commercial. But then something unexpected happens again. Human beings are beautiful, unpredictable, and windy.

A powerful and unmistakable sound produced with considerable effort from the interior of the hermitage resounds like a celestial trumpet in the direction of the valley. The organic wind instrument's resonance bounces off the cliffs and rises before dissipating into the firmament on its way to Saturn. Someone who wants to continue in solitude has just given off the most sonorous fart in history.

A monk, in every sense an artist, has found a way of expressing his opinion of international tourism without breaking his vow of silence.

★

As we travel towards the east, the original forests are exchanged for fruit trees and low bushes. Later, the scenery becomes uncultivated and cracked. Fields abandoned to the sun produce nothing but dust, yellow pastures and black smoke in abundance. On the horizon, Thrace is in flames.

In 1923 Greek and Turkish politicians reached an accord involving an exchange of populations that obligated hundreds of thousands of people to abandon their homes. The Greeks in Turkey had to exile themselves in Greece and the Turks in Greece were forced to return to the land of their ancestors. This is how they would prevent the periodic wars which arose between the two countries. However, they forgot Thrace, the last frontier of Europe.

At the end of the road is a bridge over the Maritza River, occupied by a string of stationary vehicles headed towards Istanbul. It is summer, the sky continues to shine with the brilliance of many suns and the flies have left the banks of the river to entertain themselves with us. There are no trees, there is no wind, and there are no shady places in which to seek refuge. There is also no air. The stamp says we have left Greece, but we're not in Turkey. We're in limbo, on a bridge, in No Man's Land.

I shut off the motor and get out. The pavement is scorching hot. I stretch and start to walk lazily so that my sandals don't stick. Behind me are German and French cars occupied by women that suffer the heat in silence wearing long coloured dresses. There are actual walls of trucks with stickers announcing TR, the international abbreviation for Turkey. The trucks create a little shade for groups of men seated on the road smoking and playing cards. This is not a good sign. They speak calmly, as if they're familiar with the ritual of crossing the border between two countries that continue their tradition of declaring war on each other every 50 years.

It happened during Independence. It happened again during World War I. It happened again because of Cyprus. It happened again recently because of some rocky islets in the Aegean. Tomorrow there will be a war for Thrace.

In front of the first car there's a middle-aged man who has just finished talking to a border guard. The guard is wearing his official helmet and his mounted bayonet, just in case.

"Mmm... not understanding problem, not being problem," reasons the Turkish-German in English, disorientated in No Man's Land.

"Then, why is the border closed?"

"Well, yes, is problem, perhaps. Don't know. Maybe. Greek customs, very slow, causes big line-ups in Turkey. Then, Turkey shuts down the border till cars arrive in Greece. Then, I believe, huge line-ups in Greece. Then, the Greeks work faster."

It's a strange logic. We are the pebble in the shoe, the tack in the seat, the revenge of neighbours fighting over the volume level of a television set.

An eye for an eye, a tooth for a tooth, a traffic jam for a traffic jam.

FIND ALL THE PHOTOGRAPHS FOR THIS CHAPTER AT
WWW.VIAJEROS4X4X4.COM

SADDAM'S MOUSTACHE

When the gate that prevents our entry into Turkey eventually opens, a sweaty, tired and dehydrated avalanche runs towards the immigration office. Dozens of arms push documents through the tiny window trying to get the attention of the most important man at the border: the owner of the official entry stamp. While the police try to restore order and organise a new line-up, the odour of hours spent on the bridge under the sun begins to well up in me again. I begin to distinguish the Turkish words I've jotted down on a small piece of paper, *evet, teşekkür ederim, arkadaş,* and I study the range of gestures in an attempt to decipher body language. Men take the initiative while women wait by the side; to say 'no' they raise their chin in a fleeting movement; they smile more than in Greece; we are the only ones wearing short trousers.

The customs employee has already noticed this and when we stop the van by his side he leans in the window to check out the interior.

Photo: Recess at school, village of Ishan, eastern Turkey

But he doesn't look towards the back, he looks down. He seems to be more interested in deciding if Anna's legs are legal. Then he steps back and smiles impishly, takes one of the immigration receipts, puts it in his pocket and raises the palm of his left hand towards Istanbul. Everything's in order, everything's fine.

We have hardly crossed the border when the sky becomes tinged with the colour of asphalt. The air, thick and humid, is further charged with the involuntary contribution which evaporates from our bodies. The seats darken; the remains of an unpleasantly hot day are turning into a storm. The yellow grass, crisp and tired of so much summer, asks the sky to empty itself.

To the right is the Sea of Marmara and it's not blue, it's silvery. The line which can be seen on the other side must be... Asia.

All of the thick details on the maps, all of it traced with my fingers during periods of insomnia are here and they're all true. Peninsulas, rivers and mountains, the green of the fields, the brown of the mountain ranges. We put faces to strange names stubbornly determined to confound and twist our tongues. We head towards the east, then the south, and again towards the east with only the intent of moving further away. We've been travelling for two months but my body remains disorientated, caught between leaving behind a known way of life and the start of something different, without a fixed schedule, without dates, without obligations. We're looking for something which perhaps doesn't even exist, the elusive formula that will help us prepare our declaration of independence.

After 2,000 kilometres on the road, our hands are not large enough to caress the planet's scars.

★

Istanbul, which used to be called Constantinople, Augusta Antonina, Byzantium, Lygos and Semistra, is an encyclopaedia of Turkey. A salad of hard-boiled egg-sellers standing in front of a luxury Chanel store, with a side of raw peasants scrambled with executives in a hurry at the door of a 19th century embassy. Tossed between antique

Ottoman buildings is a man who wants to charge you double because you're a foreigner and another who offers you a glass of tea because you're tired. You have to listen; everyone has something important to say.

We mix it up, and before serving, we add a touch of salt and pepper, a woman wearing a chador and a bleached blonde wearing a mini-skirt which no bearded Turkish male can ignore. We accompany this with a glass of raki on ice, an anise-flavoured liqueur made of green grapes similar to French pastis, Greek ouzo and Arabian arak. And we have it served by the street sellers of traditional pastries. *They making cakies for you! So that tourists being happy at Istanbul! Who else would it being for?*

Istanbul is a crossroads, the hope of Kyrgyz, Southern Russians, Arabs, Azeris, Bulgarians, and Georgians. For those peoples who once formed part of the Ottoman Empire, it's the doorway to Asia and the threshold of Europe. There are Westerners as well, but most only go as tourists, to visit the Grand Bazaar, Hagia Sofia and the Topkapi Palace, buy a rug and a water pipe, go to the only unisex hamam in the Muslim world, and continue speaking in any language but Turkish.

"What do I need to visit Barcelona?" is *the* question.

"I suppose a visa would be sufficient."

"Is that difficult to get?"

Ziya knows. He doesn't have any problems getting a business visa to travel by himself or with his wife to any country in the European Union. It's not enough to have an impressive bank account or property; his sons are the guarantee, the hostages that ensure they will return.

"What if I get married?" asks a Kyrgyz.

"First you have to find a woman, and women are found with love or with money."

"How much do they cost?"

★

On his 24th birthday, Ziya's mother called him into the kitchen. It was a bit odd, he hardly ever entered that part of the house, being the private domain of women. That door represented an invisible frontier where all the privileges and benefits gained by his being male and the eldest son were parked. In the kitchen he was once again a little boy, in the kitchen his mother was in charge.

The situation unsettled him and he was uncomfortable, though it did not upset him too much. He had fond memories of peeling potatoes and onions while watching the agility of his mother surrounded by pots and ladles. However, he had wanted the years to pass quickly so everyone would think of him as a man. He ended adopting the same attitude as his father: if he needed something from the kitchen, he would ask for it at the door.

This time it wouldn't be like that. He could not remain outside, away. His mother told him to enter, and not just that, before getting into the discussion, she asked that he listen.

It started with flattery, she was up to something. Among other good things, she said that he was now of age and had become a respectable man working at the factory and that she was proud he had never been in any serious trouble. Yes, there were some relatively unimportant things; throwing stones at the Turkish police in Kurdistan wasn't something shameful. He was only a rebellious 10-year-old child when he was locked up in a cell for three days during which time he cried to the point of dehydration. They released him when his father, a manufacturer of street clothes, paid someone to make the charges disappear.

The point of the talk was that he had to take on responsibilities.

Several months had passed since his father had started having conversations with Mahmut Dogan, a distant cousin with whom he had done several important business deals. He belonged to the same clan and they felt a rapport, especially when they celebrated signing a deal with a bottle of raki. That day, after talking about trousers, shipments, loads and trucks, they mentioned the possibility of consolidating family ties. And that could only be done through marriage.

Aziza was 15 years old. She had spent four years helping her mother doing housework and for a while she was in charge of everything: cooking, washing, and taking care of her father, her older and younger brothers, cleaning the house, shopping, everything. That was during The Sad Days, it was her way of not talking about the accident.

They still don't know how, but some sparks from the kitchen had caught her mother's dress on fire, turning her into a human torch. The layers of clothes had saved her chubby body, but she needed to be admitted to the hospital with serious third degree burns to her face that had turned into a mask sewn by a bad tailor. Since then she looked at the world from behind the slit of a burka. She didn't do it for her husband's benefit, or for tradition, or even for her faith in the commandments of the Holy Koran. She did it to spare others. She decided it seconds after seeing her deformed reflection in a mirror.

During those sad days Aziza took charge of the house. It was her duty. These concerns hid her joy under a seriousness that did not match her age. There was no time for dejection, and the laments were left for family reunions that became unexpected sessions of group therapy. She had to work, and she worked a lot. Now that her shadowy mother had returned to a certain normalcy, it was time to look forward. Life had to continue. A wedding, with its doses of contagious joy and festivity would be well received and beneficial to both families. And she could then take care of her own home, of her own husband. She had earned it.

Ziya sensed tradition calling him, and agreed with pride. He had spent years preparing for this moment. He knew that some day he would take charge of his father's affairs; he was the oldest of thirteen brothers, the sole heir of all the family's rights and obligations.

The dowry the family paid for the bride was the equivalent of a two-year-old cow. They took some time before having children because Aziza was still young, but they soon went to live in Istanbul.

"It's been 12 years since my first daughter was born," continues Ziya, thin, tall, with black hair and sharp features. "I celebrated it by opening my best bottle of raki with my father, who had just given me another sister."

We met them at the campground in Istanbul where they had set themselves up after the last earthquake jolted the city. By then Ziya had already taken charge of the family's textile factory: Trousers, Shirts and Jackets Bianco. He learned enough Russian, Polish and Bulgarian to extend his business into Eastern Europe while his father, the greatest man who had ever existed on the face of the Earth, continued taking care of his old clients. It had not gone badly for him.

"I respect my father a great deal. That is why I never smoke in front of him. We must respect our elders. Always. I do not allow any of my younger brothers to smoke in my presence. I'm the Big Brother, the boss after the big boss," he assures us with a tranquil look that only someone with irrefutable certainty can have.

In their house everyone has their chores: the husband takes care of the work and the woman takes care of the home. And since tradition dictates that a married man must never enter the kitchen, if the Big Brother is hungry, loyal Aziza must feed him. With a sign from his hand, one of his sisters returns to bring slices of sweet melon to accompany the raki. Being the firstborn son, he is responsible for their lives, for feeding and clothing them and for their moral guidance. For this reason he quiets them if they laugh too much and forbids them from going to dances or going out at night if he believes it's inappropriate. His sisters, almost 20 years old, obey.

His curiosity is so great he can't help ask questions about our jobs, our family, our lives and how much our *evcigim*, our "dear little house" cost. The women want to know how the wedding was, if Pablo gets angry if he's alone and hungry, if Anna also drives the van and why Pablo is washing his own clothes. At each new reply the women's faces betray a look of *I have never heard of such a thing!*

Every revolution starts with some uncomfortable questions.

The conversation barely scratches the surface of reality. The struggle to maintain a dialogue of broken words in a language which is not his or ours aggravates the loss of clarity. If you can't find a way of explaining your belief, everything seems more radical.

"We're not that different, and that's what's dangerous," suggests Anna the next day, when Ziya's sisters disappear from the campsite. We never saw them again.

Only Aziza, surrendering her life for the sake of family stability, remains with her husband.

★

Our days in Istanbul continue uncovering a powerful contest between the sun and the rain that ends in a tie. Amid the souks, mosques and forgotten palaces we forget about the theft of our belongings in Athens and we get used to living with less. It's not difficult, we have more space and the risk of having the same items stolen again is zero. On a city bus an Armenian grandfather relives with angry resignation the genocide of a century ago. On permanent display at the museum of the Topkapi Palace is a hand and part of the skull of St. John the Baptist encased in golden armour. In the next room there are reliquaries with hairs from the beard of the Prophet Mohammed, a broken mould of the imprint of his foot and a little old woman that trembles with emotion.

That last night our neighbours Ziya and Aziza invite us to a farewell dinner. After the Greek indifference, Turkish hospitality finds us unprepared.

"Before we left I would have sworn that everything was backwards, the Greeks were the good guys and that you were the bad guys," I assure them while the Asian sky lights up. "Did you see the film Midnight Express? That was bad propaganda."

On the other side of the Sea of Marmara, lightning bolts light up the coast in brilliant flashes which turn the towering minarets into missiles pointed at the sky. The lights of a giant cargo ship move towards the Bosporus and leave behind the shadows of barely visible boats. Ridiculous waves crash on the dirt beach mixed with bits of plastic and wooden fruit crates.

Big Brother knows that I live in short trousers because my long ones were stolen in Athens, and I'll find another pair when winter starts. For that reason he presents us with a couple of magnificent trousers of genuine cotton from his family's factory, with elastic waistbands and ankles. They're frightful.

Anna's are brown with white vertical lines and mine are heavenly blue with white vertical rhomboids, the latest fashion of Bianco Style in Eastern Europe. I try them on; I look like a sultan out of a cartoon. It's ideal for somnambulists, a genuine pyjama pant designed to roam the streets while asleep. And after some zucchinis and peppers stuffed with red rice, some Russian caviar and more glasses of rake with melon, Big Brother Zeya writes on a piece of paper:

> *'ben Ziya arkadas, sizleri cok seviyorum herne ovursaniz olun*
> *iyi insanlar her yerde iyi diye hatirlanirlar.*
> *Ben sizleri dahasi her zaman hatirlayacagim.*
> *Unutmayin. Ziya.'*

> *'I, your friend Ziya, love you because good people always find*
> *themselves with good people.*
> *I love you and will always be your friend.*
> *I'll never forget you. Ziya.'*

It occurs. Things happen. At times you don't realise you're crossing a line until you're on the other side.

And life will never be the same again.

Towards the end of winter we leave Istanbul. We cross over the bridge that closes the Bosphorus wound and, even though the asphalt does not change, from here on everything is new. Cape Town, South Africa, is 8,000 kilometres away as the crow flies. Curves still don't count.

Our relationship as a couple continues firmly seated by way of Insult Therapy, which has turned into a competition of ingenuity: grumpy dwarf, breast wart, infected boil, a nothing, rash, fly, disorientated fart, mange, second-hand heart, stomach ache.

Our 4x4 behaves better than we do, and hopefully will continue to do so, since we don't even know how to repair a wretched flat. Before we left we closed in four windows with sheets of aluminium, forged a good bumper out of steel, and riveted two pieces of angle iron with holes at each door to install added locks. It won't put the best thieves out of work, or the most desperate, but it does make it a bit more difficult. We installed a solar panel to recharge the battery when we camp out in the bush and an extra 75-litre fuel tank in place of where the spare tire was, which ended on the roof. Anna learned to change filters, oils and brakes in a mechanic's shop while I took an aseptic photography course. That seems enough.

The only thing we know about the future is that almost every country is connected to another by a road, and every road in the world starts at the door of our house.

We have maps that guide us towards the south, but they're maps based on faith. Conditions in Africa can change hour to hour, at any moment a tribal war can start or a flood of biblical proportions unfolds, crippling bridges and roads. A situation might develop which would not let you go forward and would not let you go back. After so many years of security, doubt is marvellous.

Around a corner three yellow and brown mottled buildings appear in the middle of a field like carrots out of Chernobyl. There is not a soul about, but there are white curtains in the windows and flowerpots on the balconies. We cross cultivated green hills and villages of half-built houses; a habitable lower floor with an upper floor of rusty beams. Market stalls overflow in disorderly waterfalls of vegetables, clothes and kitchen wares.

We stop by a gas station to load up on *uçuz mazot,* cheap Iraqi contraband diesel. The look of the fellow in charge is much like the other 35 million Turks: short, well-combed jet-black hair, thick black moustache which is trimmed daily, not the slightest hint of a beard and a bright appearance. The spitting image of Saddam Hussein.

While we fill our cups with tea, Saddam, the humane, explains that his home is 1,500 kilometres away in a city called Mardin. Every two weeks he travels there to visit his wife and two children. There's not a lot of work, but he's happy to have a job.

Twenty metres away a troop of ten men steps off a bus and fills the air with the music of clarinets, kettledrums and violins. People from the streets spontaneously form a circle and dance with their arms interlinked around a Turkish flag. It's pretty, like a movie, a cinematic nationalist propaganda film from the 1950s: happy peasants celebrating the regime.

A curious mechanic, who has the same design of moustache as the fellow in charge of the gas station, approaches and in rustic English he repeats the usual basic questions: country of origin, destination, if Turkey is beautiful. Later, without saying anything, he moves away then returns. In his hands he carries a large round loaf of bread.

"This is Turkish bread. That is not," he says, pointing with contempt to the baguette that Anna has just sliced open. A few metres away, the passengers of the bus dance like marionettes with tangled strings.

Something happens. Ten minutes after appearing in a remote gas station two Saddam Hussein clones offer us some tea and bread, basic hospitality, the least that a mass murderer can do to begin redeeming his sins. Fresh baked bread and sweet tea, without razor blades, without hemlock or napalm. *Chew with confidence. Drink, drink, I will bring you more.*

I look around, searching amid the passers-by that slow down when they come near us. I'm afraid of discovering the greatest criminals of the last century living a decent life. Honest. Simple. Ordinary people with glasses and a bit of a belly who help their neighbours take care of the kids. The common folk, without vices or delusions of grandeur, the type that would knock on your door to ask for a cup of sugar.

Adolf Hitler, authorised propane distributor further down the road. Idi Amin Dada, the best steakhouse in the neighbourhood; nobody knows where he buys such exquisitely tender meat. Pol Pot, Stalin and Pinochet, the most hospitable guys in the world, who innocently offer up a tray of traditional pastries. Slobodan Milosevic lights up with a genuine smile, not forced, when he confesses having an honest interest in finding a faster way of returning lands to their original inhabitants. Ceausescu is laughing with Dr. Mengele who is telling pro-Semitic jokes. Or anti-Aryan ones. A certain Leopold of Belgium shows us some rubber trays with prosthetic hands, feet and arms, specifically designed to repair the atrocities caused by machetes and landmines in African conflicts. I don't know, they all seem too real.

Anastasio Somoza gives us a wink.

Trujillo invites us to his home.

Robert Mugabe, Radovan Karadzic and Henry Kissinger are stopping people on the street. They are collecting signatures for Amnesty International. Osama bin Laden folds paper airplanes for children. He lets them pull on his beard.

An old man named Jorge Videla comes near walking with a stick. He looks inoffensive, kinder than Mother Teresa of Calcutta. Kinder than Lady Di, may God take care of her in heaven. He cheers Saddam, who serves us up another tea. He stumbles while dragging his feet towards a chair to rest in the shade. He can barely stand. When he sits down, he turns on a radio and brings it close to his ear. They are rebroadcasting the final game of the '78 Football World Cup in Argentina. Later, Grandpa Jorge puts his hand in a bag and pulls out round loaves of bread to feed bands of grey pigeons, harmless flocks that fly in. They land on his body. They start feeding right on his legs, on his arms and shoulders. They get excited and jump on his head, and he disappears.

★

With the fading light of the day we discover the entrance to an abandoned quarry, a good place to spend the night. There are no guardhouses, or fences, machinery or nearby villages or recent tracks, just a three-quarter moon and thousands of shining lights in the sky. It looks like the ceiling of a supermarket at Christmas. Yes, I have too much city in my blood.

We dine on a vegetable sandwich: bread, tomato, onion, cucumber, olive oil and salt. Then we move the water containers and the bags to the passenger seat, we unfold the mattress over the horizontal drawers, we install the curtains on all the windows, and we brush our teeth. Two minutes brushing our canines. We read. We bet our chores on card games. We study Turkish. We look over a map and decide which line we'll be following tomorrow. And we close our eyes about the same time as chickens do, eight or nine at night.

In a few seconds three hours pass, it's almost midnight and there's a knocking on the door of our house, our van.

"Ey Messieur!!"

I wake with a start, the imprint of a wrinkled sheet of paper on my face. The fading flashlight makes a few centimetres of the sheets glow yellow. Outside, the darkness is complete, the moon has disappeared and only the heavenly lights illuminate the shadow that moves from window to window. That flattens his nose against the glass to look inside. That caresses the sides of the van.

Where did this guy come from?

"What's going on..." murmurs Anna with her eyes still closed. The bed moves. Then more bumps resound.

"Messieur!!! Ey Messieur!!!"

Someone is knocking on the door of our house at midnight. The slow drowsiness disappears beneath a release of adrenaline directly to the heart, which speeds up. TUMTUM. It's a distorted ball against the floor TUMTUM that is pounding on your chest TUMTUM, runaway horses and boxers TUMTUM, ghosts and demons TUMTUM, because no one is waiting for you TUMTUM, and no one knows you TUMTUM, because you don't dance on a loose tightrope TUMTUM, you dance on a thin razor's edge.

All the chemical alarms in my body react, alerted by what should never happen. I put my index finger to my lips to ask Anna to remain silent and I look for the marine flare gun. I would rather not use it, but I know I have to fire at chest height. TUMTUM. I remove the red cap off the muzzle. I look for the silver ring.

Will he be alone? TUMTUM.

A second of silence lasts considerably longer than a second of sound. Complete silence is striking. I follow the intruder through the beaten glass. He's stout but short; his silhouette is outlined by the white chalk walls of the quarry. Yes, he's alone. He looks like he's alone. TUM- TUM. He's carrying a stick in his hand and has a moustache on his face, Saddam by night. John Smith, José Pérez, the anonymous drunk, the unknown Turk transformed into Mister Hyde.

He turns; he circles with the agility of a ghost. Why do almost all Turks wear that same moustache? TUMTUM. He looks at the windows, he tries to get through the glass. We're surrounded by just one man.

"Hey *Messieur!!!!*"

Anna looks at me, scrunched up in her sleeping bag, leaning against the map pasted on the wall. She has her body in Asia and her head in Africa. Her elbows are new giant peninsulas in the oceans. TUMTUM. The line drawn in black is still too short, TUMTUM.

I hate nocturnal visits in remote places. Only extraterrestrials are welcome. I want him to leave. If I say something in Spanish he will not understand.

Tired and sleepy, without thinking for a second about the animal nature of it, my instinct responds, I give out a mighty roar TUMTUM, a shout torn from my bestiary.

"Wrrrrrooooooaaaaaaaaaaaahhhhhh!!!!!!!"

Let's return to the Stone Age.

"No problem!!" shouts Saddam by night. But he flings a rock to check out the roof.

TUMTUM my heart beats faster TUMTUM.

He crouches again to look underneath TUMTUM where the propane stove sleeps TUMTUM, with the stick or cane TUMTUM scraping the body of our house TUMTUM, and he goes ahead TUMTUM where the water freezes at night TUMTUM, he checks out our bumper TUMTUM lost or curious or something worse TUMTUM, dangerous.

TUMTUM TUMTUM.

I turn on the high beams. They light up the mutilated spectre of a clumsy ghost. He does not have a head, he does not have legs, and he has a heavy stick in his hand. I lean on the horn.

"No problem!! No problem!!!" he shouts again before lifting his hands TUMTUM and finally TUM he starts to walk away.

When I finally get back to sleep I have too many nightmares. I dream that I've awakened and we've never left Barcelona; that I have to sell a new advertising campaign to a bank dressed only in a loincloth; the whole world, men, women, children and dogs have the same beard as Saddam Hussein. It's frightening.

★   ★

Dawn finds me with open eyes. Outside there's nobody, the quarry is empty. There are no footprints of men with sticks. I look at Anna; she does not have a moustache. We have a nervous breakfast, outside the uterus that protected us during the night, prisoners of a new feeling of insecurity. We put back the water containers in their place and return to the road before giving paranoia a chance to set in.

What happened last night?

We cross the beating heart of Anatolia, surrounded by flocks of wolves disguised as sheep. Sinister forests and sharpened ridges turn into intimidating mountains. It's fear, no doubt, fear of stray bullets and of that which should never occur. We avoid Ankara and take curves and infinite counter curves surrounded by fields of crops. A tombstone appears to be planted amidst a fertile patch of corn. There are no clouds in this transparent sky.

The fear.

At the outer limits of Cappadocia the scenery turns so arid that it's discouraging. There are kilometres of charred, cracked dirt of such a light colour that it starts to look ghostly white. Dirt without life, dead, abandoned, turned into bone dust. TUMTUM.

At a fork in the road there is an old man wearing navy-blue trousers, light blue shirt and a captain's hat. He doesn't exist, it's my nerves, and it's a hallucination. His white moustache, which starts in one of the wrinkles that quarter his face, can't hide his smile. He doesn't look like any known Saddam. When Anna asks him about Mustafa Pasha, he signals confusedly forward.

"Yes! Okay! Mustafa Pasha!"

Mustafa Pasha is an ancient Greek town. It has old churches, mosques and madrasas, old Mediterranean houses and troglodyte houses, old Ottoman pillars, old aqueducts, old bars and old stores. Everything is old, the wooden shelves are covered in dust, everything is covered in dust. The excavated houses on the mountainside crumble out into patios criss-crossed with wind-blown clothes. Its original name was Sinasos but after the exchange of populations with Greece, the Turks decided to change it for something with a more Oriental sound. And nothing could be more Oriental than Mustafa Pasha.

"Have you heard of Gomede?" asks the town's shopkeeper while we find some Turkish money to pay for the tomatoes, eggs and dust.

"Goreme?"

"No, Gomede, another ancient valley, with houses carved into the mountains, like Goreme, Ortaysar or Ilhara, but without tourists. It's our valley, very close by."

Fifteen minutes later we stop in front of a throat of vertical walls, splashed with window-like holes. They are not just holes, but actual windows. A table, carved right into the floor, peeks out from a naturally formed balcony above the treetops. Some walls have symmetrically placed rectangles, shelves. The water from the stream, which in winter must be abundant, has eroded the stone until it forms a tunnel which avoids a pronounced curve. Then I turn and see the blue shirt of the keeper, who has been watching us with a smile: it's the friendly old man with the captain's hat.

Bahri Kashar lives in Mustafa Pasha. He's 49 years old, but he looks a great deal older. He works seven days a week and when he can't find a tractor to take him to his troglodyte workplace, he walks. It's that simple. He's grey-haired, and despite his cirrhosis, he always has two bottles on hand to celebrate coincidences. He fills our glasses with raki, his glass with orange Fanta, and he raises his voice.

"Raki, şerefe!"

"Salud!"

We are the company that he has been missing in the solitude of this valley. His eyes shine when we speak the basic language of our fifteen Turkish words, though he understands the intent of our gestures. Our spirits communicate directly and they leave us with only our clumsy outward motions.

"Harita" he teaches us by pointing to a map before repeating all the numbers past ten, *onbir, on iki, on üc…* and the barriers continue to fall.

When Anna asks about his wife he only says *tomb*. If you speak the same language you can say "she died some years ago" or "she's passed away" or "she's gone off with the milkman." But when there are just a few words, you have to choose the clearest so that no doubt remains. Tomb. Sometimes he repeats what he hears and laughs. He already knows that if someone tries to get in without paying, like us, he has to say 'take it easy bro'. If something falls, we pick it up saying 'no probs'.

"Take it easy bro, no probs" he repeats, smiling again.

Every morning Bahri waits on a sofa carved into the rock for the few daily tourists. Indeed, all the furniture is carved out of the rock: tables, chairs, sofas, shelves, the bed. He only wakes up when he hears

Grandpa Bahri cooking outside his refuge in Gomede Valley, Capadocia

an engine or the first murmurs of admiration before the spectacle of his pot-marked valley. At the end of the visit he always takes out the bottle of raki, that way visitors find it harder to leave. If he has batteries he takes out an enormous radio cassette that plays saturated music complete with original crackling. If he gets too bored, he looks for his rifle and practices target shooting unfortunate lizards.

The place of honour in his cave is occupied by a huge Turkish flag and a framed picture of Ataturk, the father of Turkey. On each side are some rustic local carpets, surrounded by the typical tapestries you would find at Chinese restaurants anywhere in the world, with reindeer happy to be reindeer and mountains sewn in brilliant colours. The shelves store cheese and yogurt prepared by his mother with the milk from her own cows, tulip-shaped glasses and a tin with plastic flowers. When a storm leaves him isolated he survives thanks to an old wood stove that pumps heat from the centre of the cave, from the centre of his refuge.

At midday Bahri picks some tomatoes from his garden and finds a package of *bulgur pilaf,* a wheat couscous. Anna looks for her grandmother's pot in the van, a couple onions, oil and some red peppers, and together they start cooking on a small wood fire. They understand each other so well speaking languages that are so different that they finish flaying me in Turkish, English, Spanish, Catalan and deaf mute. Bahri is funny.

"Hotel. Hotel Yabadabadu" he repeats while pointing to the other side of the valley.

"Hotel Yabadabadu?" I ask.

He crosses his arms on his chest, closes his eyes, opens his mouth and lets his head fall like a dead marionette.

"Hotel Yabadabadu, tomb."

The Flintstones, of course, super stars in Cappadocia.

The sepulchres of the troglodyte church, aligned like bunk beds, have been sacked of bones and treasures. What is left of the altar is barely separated from the wall, and a pair of columns fused to the floor supports the vaulted ceiling. The walls, covered in religious paintings of Christ and various saints, have had their faces scratched off by the Muslim invasion that came from the south. Only Allah, God, has the power to create a man and give him a face.

Right next to the door of the temple begin the houses, an incredible collection of tunnels that join rooms excavated upwards, downwards, and to the sides. There's a corner with the sooty remains of a bonfire. A bowl-shaped hole devoid of grapes connects a channel dried of any wine and falls into another earthenware bowl full of dust. The doors are giant wheels made of stone. On almost every wall are long narrow cavities, almost like a niche in a catacomb; beds for the living. The floor, worn by footsteps, inclines towards the centre and, despite the fact the first rooms are quite large, the confined quarters make me shiver.

The ancients lived here.

The inhabitants of Cappadocia became moles before the Middle Ages. Their country was a place of transit, war and pillage for all the armies determined to conquer Istanbul, Jerusalem or Bagdad. Two thousand years ago, the only way of surviving was to be in exile, or under the floor of soft rock that could be carved with a stick. This is how Cappadocian subterranean cities started, enormous anthills with hidden doors and ventilation systems, labyrinthine spaces capable of hiding and feeding up to 10,000 people for six months.

Bahri leaves his troglodyte office before darkness falls and the moon starts to reflect strange patterns on the walls of the valley. It's not pleasant returning home walking amid ochre-coloured walls dyed with a spectral white, the colour the dead take on after they've been gone for a few hours, before the make-up, the lipstick, and the rouge to the cheeks.

Two hours later a round moon parodies the work of the sun. At the other side of the valley the shadows stretch slowly on the veil of the wall. Monsters appear, desperate mouths, broken teeth, disfigured faces, empty sockets, blind eyes that disappear and rise further on.

They move.

Not a great deal of time has passed from when the caves were still inhabited and almost everything was due to the will or anger of the gods. The daytime was life. The night-time was the domain of the wolf, the domain of panic.

During those times only the flicking light of oil lamps and cooking fires intoxicated the air with black smoke. There were no lanterns or flashlights or firearms to strike from afar. Only lances and faith to conquer the darkness of the world, the hungry demons, the devil's long shadow.

Summer was a temperate spring: open flowers, trees loaded with fruit, wheat field, wild barley and innocent rabbits out of a Walt Disney movie who believed the pot was only for a warm bath. When winter arrived the inhabitants had to protect themselves from the cold. The openings to the cave didn't have doors, the windows were not insulated with double-paned glass. All the food was buried in the snow, dead or alive.

Wild animals descended from the mountains to hunt children.

Winter could only be survived.

I listen to the distant howls of dogs or wolves; not the same thing. September has hardly started, the mountains are still free of snow, and leaves still cling to trees with serenity and calm, without despair.

As we continue towards the north, the arid beige once again gives way to the juicy green of the mountains around the Black Sea. The old *dolmuş,* overstuffed minibuses that painfully drag themselves over the asphalt, replace the modern air-conditioned motor-coach buses that used to pass us at great speed. In the north of Turkey there are few tourists.

We slowly drive through the main streets of villages inhabited by seated-under-the-sun grandfathers and we draw a lot of attention. They don't understand what we're doing here when young people are going to Istanbul or Ankara because there are no jobs, and their place as an unemployed person is filled by other young folks that arrive from the fields. But times are tough, now it's difficult to find work even in

Istanbul. Immigrants without papers from ex-Soviet Union countries sweat from sunrise to sunset for less money. In their homeland there is even less work.

In front of a farm, a procession accompanies a new bride covered in white veils. The only man bangs a drum while thirty women laugh and celebrate the ritual, ignoring the humid wind that predicts rain. Two men greet us or try to stop us, I'm not sure. Later, a vagabond wrapped in threadbare rags dances while opening his cloth wings. He's brown, intensely green and leafy, like a forest.

At a mountain pass, houses held up with wooden posts spread their legs to let impossible rivers flow. Currents of moist air lift the skirts of hanging plants to reveal an embarrassment of rotting wood. We stop by another gas station that sells Iraqi petrol and the man in charge invites us for more tea. When he brings the glasses, his voice becomes a whisper, as if his throat had been closed in an official attempt to not emit sounds. I don't understand the mystery until he pronounces kilise and repeats the action of putting on bracelets. Many armies passed through here and left their dead dressed up underground, around the churches. Bahri's history lesson returns: you're poor, you're lucky, you find an intact tomb and you go to Germany, the promised land of the Turks. It's the dream of the man in charge of a gas station that sells contraband diesel.

The city of Tokat is an ancient Hittite-Midian-Persian-Roman-Mongol-Byzantine-Greek-Ottoman place, the site where Julius Caesar pronounced *vini, vidi, vici.*

Hardly have we parked when we are surrounded by a small group of curious people. They're determined we must climb the *kale*, the castle, a pile of shapeless blocks two hundred metres up a mountain, the only standing testimony to glory and conquest. The pride of Tokat. Even the postman stops us and in five emotional seconds repeats his entire English vocabulary while pointing to the summit. "Hello, welcome, friend." It's been months since we've received our last piece of mail, and the excitement of tearing an envelope to find the phone bill or some special junk mail offer has died away. "Castle, beautiful, welcome."

When there's a will, it's easy to be understood.

We forget about the ruins and look for streets guarded by wooden houses. Some children look at us with curiosity, others start to shout "Tourist! Tourist!" I'm not sure if they are calling us or raising the alarm. Some young women peer at us from behind the embroidered curtains of their homes, the older ones follow us with their eyes, stern, sullen, immutable.

We're strangers, we dress differently, our faces belong somewhere else far away. Our history is different: the build-up of sacrifices, coincidences, rituals, migrations, television programmes, unexpected births, weddings, crisis, assassinations and joys have drained into us and have taken another route, just as long as theirs. We were separated at some moment in history, and today we meet again.

A distant cousin with a lost look in her eyes follows us repeating "hello hello good night, what is your name?" It's madness. For the first time we suffer *Copito de Nieve* Syndrome* , the white foreigner that comes to observe and ends up being observed, and followed, and commented on, pointed out, studied. We're strangers, exotic animals, white apes.

The official version states that Copito de Nieve, the albino gorilla captured in Equatorial Guinea who served a life sentence at the zoo in Barcelona, took on his destiny willingly. The legends which circulate amid the cages assure us of something else: during his moments of anger and rebellion, Copito would launch his excrements against the glass which separated him from the public.

Today, nobody has to turn on the television to prove that in the west, men and women walk hand in hand, that she wears her hair loosely and uncovered, that he has a beard like an Imam but wears short trousers. Here men walk hand in hand with men and women hold other women's hands. The sexes do not mix.

And yet we are not far from home.

---

*Copito de Nieve: Snowflake.

We pass by an old abandoned Turkish bath, Ottoman temples in a state of decomposition, and the shell of an old *caravanserai,* a refuge for caravans. We walk into a trouser factory. For a month I have lived showing my calves, and it's starting to get cold. And either because of vanity or self-esteem, I don't dare wear the powder-blue pyjamas with rhomboids that Big Brother gave me.

When I walk out on the street again with my legs covered, I am confident that I will be a bit less visible. Anna gathers her hair. She misses the sympathetic spontaneity of Bahri as well as the sense of anonymity. She would like to walk quietly for a while, disappear, become invisible.

We confidently take a few steps on the cobbled street, but some children appear through a window and start yelling.

"Eh! Hello! Tourist, tourist! E-eh! Hello! Hello!"

We escape again. We detour through the narrowest streets, the ones which appear to be the most deserted, we take unlikely routes, but they all end in front of faces filled with surprise.

We go around another corner and a group of women stop talking to look at us. Anna picks up her pace and stops before a white house, below a string of red peppers hanging from a rope. And then, she breaks down.

But something extraordinary happens: those same women, covered in black dresses from head to toe, come up and gather her tears. Just by saying *arkadaş* and *aile* in *Isbania* they understand that she misses her friends, her family, separated by 3,000 kilometres of road and nostalgia. Distance is the toll paid by travellers.

All the repressed emotions caused by our obvious cultural differences spill out on Anna. A few anonymous arms break the cultural frontier; they gently get her up and take her towards the landing of a doorway. Emotions do not need a passport. While a young girl hurries to get a glass of water, the circle closes. After so many centuries apart, a distant aunt, an adoptive mother, takes her in her arms and caresses tenderly.

★

The hamam experience leaves you beat up but happy. It's the closest thing to getting your arms and legs ripped out of their sockets and being reassembled after each part is put through a high-pressure tunnel wash. It relaxes and cleans us, exactly what we need.

Our guidebook says that the hamam has its origins in the Roman baths, and Tokat is an especially good place to experience this intense cleansing: 'The Ali Pasha Hamami, built in 1352, is the granary that feeds the demand for professionals in the Turkish baths of Istanbul.' Great, I suppose that's why I imagined a row of masseurs, stout and with thick moustaches, awaiting the arrival of their customers. But no, the only masseur in this gloomy hamam is so thin and gaunt that he looks malnourished.

I take off nearly all my clothes in a small room with wooden walls and I enter the empty showers with a towel wrapped around my waist. It's the only logical thing to do: I have been cleaning myself with baby towelettes for the last ten days.

When I start relaxing below the marvellous stream of warm water I feel a finger running over my spine. I'm almost naked in a bath used exclusively by men with moustaches who are also almost naked. And their moustaches, Saddam's moustache, is the same moustache as Freddy Mercury's!

It's the Malnourished Masseur. He motions me to follow him and seats me on a giant slab of warm marble. He removes the wrapping on a new bar of soap, foams it up and starts scrubbing my arms with a giant mitten. He is going to bathe me.

I would like to believe that the long dark strings which descend when he passes the sandpaper textured glove over my skin are only accumulated grime, but I'm not so sure. These are not the loving baths that my mother gave me when I was a child. I try to relax with my back against the wall, but the Malnourished Masseur grabs a leg and starts scrubbing it like a fanatic polishing a trophy. He soaps up my foot, my knee, behind my knee, my thigh, and then he changes legs; we're champions. I become unstained, my arms, my neck and back lose their filth, colour or skin. I'm rosy again.

When he finishes snapping in my arms and screwing my legs back on, he drags me submissively to where a fire warms a circular marble base of some ten square metres. He throws a bucket of water to clean off the dried sweat, I lie down and he begins again. This time the heat, the contortions and the cracking of my bones sink me into a profound drowsiness.

I close my eyes. Just as I am about to fall asleep, I feel him grab my unprepared head with his hands.

"Massage *okey*?" he asks.

"Okay…" I reply in a low committed voice, before feeling and hearing, feeling the brusque turn of my head and hearing the terrifying cracking of half my cervical vertebrae.

"Tip two million *okey*?" he asks again emphatically, before turning my head to the other side. It's the perfect moment to extort his tip. Whatever mistake might well have been an accident.

"Tip *okeyokeyokey*!" I quickly respond. Absolutely. Sure.

After surviving these *cracks* I lose myself for two marvellous hours of oblivion and catalepsy. There are only four of us walking between the sauna and the cold water showers, from the cold showers to the hot marble and I forget what's next. You recline, you focus your eyes on the little holes in the ceiling that let little rays of sunlight through and when you become aware of it, five minutes or an hour might have passed. It's hypnosis by way of relaxation. Your arms dismantle themselves and fall to the sides. The filtered light leaves you semi-conscious. Nothing serves as a timepiece. Nobody has anything else to do.

Time has no meaning.

Limbo is a hamam.

Anna is waiting at the door. She tells me that women enter in pairs because there is no masseuse. Mothers and daughters, sisters and friends soap themselves up, wash their hair and scrub their backs with the sandpaper mitten. They throw cold water on each other amidst giggles and bites of fresh fruit.

The only window, in front of the receptionist's desk, frames a view of an incredibly blue sky over a grey brick wall.

That's why we travel, to repeatedly surprise ourselves.

"Thanks for letting me continue to enjoy the show," I say in Spanish when I give him the promised tip on pain of an accidental broken neck.

Though he does not understand all my words, the Malnourished Masseur smiles like God.

★

Sometimes life begins to seem like something you dreamed. You wrap yourself in a newly uncovered skin, fresh and bloodied, or better, you pull your eyes out and see yourself from the shoes of a stranger. What you see doesn't fit with the day-to-day routine of a year ago. Or even of a month ago. You expect to wake up any minute because it's absurd. That quagmire of fire in your hands, that insane happiness, that daily excitement, that energy that flows with strength from your guts was not a part of your normal everyday life. At least, not the everyday life you knew. Something happened; perhaps it seemed like a hasty decision, or a detour taken through boredom, an accident. You do not know how you arrived there, but you cross new situations and you absorb changes of pace, curious stares, surprises, strange words, traffic jams, short cuts and absences. You begin to learn again. Something has started to change and now you have no idea how it will end.

What happens is so extraordinary that you can't believe it: dreams and reality have fused in an embrace. They have gone away to live together.

★

If you travel slowly, everything is clearer. People's expressions speak of happiness, discouragement and an infinite number of stops along the way, like back in your old neighbourhood. You take the curves with a deliberate softness, it's not necessary to go quickly, no one is waiting, you don't have to return at any given time.

Anna turns on the radio: the van is filled with words that sound like endless equations. Something other than warm air comes through the window as we head north-east, even though our route is towards the south. *We'll find more curves.* The sides of the road are covered with tea plantations, almonds, tobacco, cherries and honeycombs. At last there's time to get lost and fill in the blank spaces.

You pass a truck loaded with five workers sitting on a flat deck, their inert legs hang over a short tailgate. They look like dwarf puppets. In another fleeting village you discover a mechanical Frankenstein, a homemade two wheeled wooden cart welded to the handlebar of half a motorcycle, which asthmatically wheezes onwards in front of a row of sexless naked mannequins. While the vanguard of winter rips the clothing off the trees, you slip through deep and shady valleys and fall into a giant pot. The Black Sea receives you in its greyness, and the clouds that are reflected in the water threaten to descend further and squash you against the ground.

Sometimes it's not easy to find a place to sleep. The fields are fenced, the road is being repaired, there are no gas stations or any way of getting to a deserted beach. Spending the night by the side of some secondary road without a forest means too much exposure. We reject the only hotel we find, filled with Russians and Kazakhs at a rate of a 135 absurd euros a night and we turn off into a narrow road. Through the mist appear two ghosts disguised as old men in dark coats. A donkey walks between them keeping time to the rhythm. I make some gestures, it's cold, but they laugh and disappear. Then we arrive in Beliçe.

"We're looking for a place to sleep," I practice a bit of Turkish, a bit of English, with a couple of adolescents seated next to the small mosque.

"Here? Okay? No problem?" I ask gesturing with my hands.

They don't understand me.

I try again.

"We're aliens from a freaky far-off planet that's 3,500 kilometres away in a straight line. We come in peace to study your customs and your civilization. Do you have any problem if we experiment on you while we sleep here?"

That doesn't work either. An old man approaches craning his neck and offers us figs. We are welcome, nothing ever happens here.

Meanwhile, balconies and windows begin to fill up with women and children. There's a spectacle today. Another old man comes near and points out that in case of emergency, we can use the bathrooms in the mosque. It's almost three in the afternoon and through the speakers directed at each of the cardinal compass points, the call to prayer begins.

Five neighbours walk energetically down the street towards the ablution fountain to purify themselves. They rinse their mouths, they breathe water up their noses, they wash their faces, their heads, the inside of their ears, the nape of their necks, feet, hands and arms. Only then do they disappear behind the door of the mosque. Once they have finished their prayers they approach us smiling.

"Hosgeldiniz," they say lighting up the words with their white teeth. "Welcome," they repeat.

Beliçe is a village surrounding a small cove below the only road that borders the Black Sea. At the intersection there are no signs with its name, consequently, it doesn't exist.

A few years ago a storm that passed only into local history produced a torrent that destroyed houses, bridges and swept away the almond trees. All of them. The sea daringly covered the beach with rocks. The village was declared a disaster area. Since then, the only way to subsist has been by fishing, or travelling to work every day in the nearest town.

In Beliçe almost everyone decided to fish. Late in the afternoon all the men arrive at the beach, whirl fishing lines with hooks over their heads, and launch them into the water. After a few seconds they pull in the lines with a jerking motion. On one rock there is the Imam of the mosque, some 40 or 50 years old and almost bald, with his short-sleeved shirt and his worn black trousers folded up to his knees. By his side, two 50-year-old brothers who live with a cow and a woman who is always smiling, are conversing. A bit further on there is a fat little boy who wants to be a hairdresser when he grows up but at the moment is entertaining himself by mimicking dogs, cows and cars that won't start. There's a young girl with a baby in each arm and her husband who doesn't hide the fact that he detests our presence. And there's Hassan, the Maniac, who is 16 years old and is going at the same speed as the entire town put together. The charge of adrenaline in his blood must be significantly greater than normal. At sunset he takes us to a corner of the beach and celebrates our encounter by burning a tire. When he feels the embers below his feet he shouts "Problem! Problem!"

Hassan needs a girlfriend.

The first morning the Imam invites us for breakfast with his family. He has two daughters and everyone is happy to share the table. They hardly speak English, and we hardly speak Turkish. We communicate in the language of loose words, gestures and smiles.

I knew the day would arrive when sitting at a regular table, just four legs and a flat surface, I would need to relearn to eat and talk in a foreign culture, neither better nor worse, just different. And there I was, sharing long silences, broken by the goodwill of the eldest daughter who refills our cups with tea, while the Imam and his wife encourage us to continue eating. Raising a plate with olives is an invitation. Refilling a plate with humus is a maxim. Slicing up more cheese is a manifesto.

I still need practice to eat my food with my right hand and without cutlery; to use the left hand, the dirty hand, the one they use to clean themselves in the bathroom with or without toilet tissue, would be a grave offence.

What surprises me most is how normal the Imam is. He does not talk about Allah, he does not bless the food, there are no prayers or visible signs of religion in his new house. He is not an official ambassador, he does not wear an uniform like Catholic priests. He dresses like everyone else in the village and nothing distinguishes him from the rest. When we finish breakfast he offers us a cigarette. Then his wife scolds him with a couple of words and reminds him of his doctor's advice. The Imam blushes, he's human.

At midday the women join up at the beach like bees around Anna. Sometimes they stutter out questions filled with strange mono-syllables but most of the time they spend watching -- digesting the expressions, the movements, even the crossing of legs. Later they take a boat and row offshore, though they are still tied to land by their children. It's been five years since the school closed, a decaying shell facing the small bay. With less than ten families, there was no alternative but to send them off each day to study at the nearest town, where some of them also found work.

When the sun approaches the horizon we go to the house of The Two Brothers and The Woman Who Smiles. Today they have spent considerably more time launching their fish lines to be able to offer us an abundant dinner. She welcomes us, dressed in her best smile, in a yellow room darkened by the passage of time. The walls are covered with pictures taken from magazines: torrential rivers, green forests and villages with tranquil waters framed in the same brown tone as the doors. Through the window we see the sun setting over the Black Sea.

The water merges with the sky, the first star appears and the Imam again calls out over the loud-speakers at the mosque. The lights on the fish boats merge with the North Star. The universe unfolds and we leave the Milky Way. Tonight we'll dine in outer space.

After two hours of epileptic conversations we return to the van. We have hardly opened the door when a new Saddam appears, this time it's Saddam in pyjamas. He proceeds to grab us by the arm and drag us towards his house. He is not sleepwalking, he's awake and just as sleepy as us. There's also no discussion possible, our opinion is irrelevant. His wife and daughters want to have a visit from the foreigners who arrived at the village. He has to obey. We do too.

It's now Anna's turn to be sociable, and I lose myself in the confusing twinkles of Turkish television. I don't understand a word, but it doesn't matter. At times my mind returns to the room and I discover that the eldest daughter, replete with make-up behind her chador and with a long cloak that reaches her ankles but with a sexy cut up to her knees, is a hairdresser. Her mother and sister sporadically work at a tea plantation. They bring another infusion, another tray with cherries and pieces of green apples; we must eat, we must drink. How do you say in Turkish 'I don't have any room left in my stomach?' As we move away from our civilisation, hospitality becomes an unwritten rule shown and practised with religious enthusiasm.

The next morning I decide to try my luck at fishing. One of The Two Brothers launches his fishing line without bait and hands it to me. I gather it rapidly with my left hand, while I imitate the short jerks with my right hand. At the end of the hook there's a silvery sargana, a relative of the long and skinny fish on which we dined last night. I'm impressed. The only thing I have ever been able to hook in my almost non-existent life as a fisherman are sardine tins at a supermarket. I look at the thin, slippery trophy: the hook, which should be going through the mouth of the fish, is instead hooked on his back. This does not seem fair.

It doesn't matter. With my confidence affirmed by my exploits, I decide to launch the line myself. I fling it around over my head, as powerfully as a spaceship, as intensely as a combat helicopter, rapidly and lightly like a hummingbird, I release: it falls about 10 metres away, not bad for a beginner. I gather it again but the hook is empty. It doesn't matter, it started out empty.

I try it again, I concentrate, this time it must reach further, better, forward. David conquers Goliath again and fishes another defenceless minnow. When I let the fishing line go, looking towards the horizon, the sea, be careful Neptune! I notice through the right corner of my eye that those who are watching me, half the town, start to run away.

As we ascend the plateau over the Coast of Rize, the frequency of trees begins to diminish. About ten kilometres from the Black Sea they disappear completely. Only bare land is left, badly faced, that slides slowly towards the road. More than a century ago the Russians razed these forests and organised enormously long caravans to send the wood to St. Petersburg, the old capital of the Tsars. The landscape changed, but the ancient crumbling Armenian and Georgian churches still remain.

Ishan is another of those forgotten villages outside the tourist route. It's close to the ridge of a mountain and it's only remembered because of the remains of a temple with some broken inscriptions. The rest is beautiful, but it's not in any guide. Undulating dirt roads surround simple houses, two gloomy stores and a Muslim cemetery consisting of thin white slabs of stone next to a cliff. Behind the village are all the trees that did not grow in the valley.

The schoolchildren, miniature men dressed in trousers, ties and hand-me-down jackets, leave their classroom running and surround us during recess. The girls are more discrete. They sit on a long bench and dissect those small gestures they've never seen at home. They discuss us in low voices, huddled together, bringing their hands up to their mouths to cover their words. They observe.

Finally, one of them gathers their courage and approaches. She puts her hands into her pockets and offers us two apples. Could these be her snack? When we stop at the start of another valley a peasant comes towards us with arms laden with peaches. We camp near a river and a fisherman presents us with three fish that still gasp desperately in the air. The owner of another gas station pulls us out of our seats and puts still more tea in front of our noses. This is too much tea, I'm turning yellow.

Amid all of this squandering of hospitality we start crossing the paths of truck caravans belonging to the Turkish army. The first roadchecks begin, set up by heavily armed rookie soldiers. They just need to file their teeth to keep them sharp. We've arrived in Kurdistan, a country divided between Turkey, Syria, Iran and Iraq, permanently longing for independence.

Kars is a city where you would not want to spend more time than absolutely necessary. The rise of military actions against the PKK, the guerrilla fighters of the Kurdistan Worker's Party, have transformed it into two parallel bodies, twins that occupy the same place. The streets are patrolled by military police in jeeps and by the civic police in cars labelled *polis karakolu*.

There are military ambulances and civilian ambulances, cantinas, stores, and even telephones exclusively for civilians or the military. The recruits, invariably sporting crew cuts, repeat their evening walks in groups of two, five or ten. They always stop at the same window displays, the same cantinas and the same telephone. Civilians cover the same route but stop at different shop windows, different cantinas and different telephones. The two towns live together, superimposed, but only ever meet in the brothels of the Natashas, Russian women that arrived with perestroika. As a result, since 1992, most Turkish women involved in the world's oldest profession dye their hair blonde.

One of the most important tasks of the Turkish army is to enforce the constitution. They have already intervened on occasions when the government threatened to impose religious or party interests. That's why it's the most respected institution in the country. But that only happens in Turkish Turkey. In Kurdistan people want the military to go away.

I drive around distractedly watching the streets, looking for a secure place to park for the night. A garrisoned town is a safe bet if you want to get lots of attention. The tree-lined streets appear quiet. We could sleep at a service station, though who has not seen those lovely balls of flame in a movie, brilliant and ambitious, expanding like a breast of fire when fuel deposits explode?

Suddenly the car in front of me screeches to a stop. My feet and my reflexes don't respond, neither do the brakes, perhaps I'm going too fast or it's the fault of the Earth that's accelerating.

We crash.

A man gets out, bothered but calm, to examine the latest wrinkle in his trunk. His official Saddam moustache moves from side to side repeating words which I would prefer not to understand. A passer-by repeats *"no problem no problem no problem"*, like some old English teacher's parrot. In the stagnant air only murmurs circulate, tongue-twisters. Now what?

Five minutes later a thin policeman with an annoyed expression appears. He examines the vehicles. He wants my passport, my driver's licence and wants me to accompany him to the police station. I think I may have found a place to spend the night.

I go through the door not knowing what can happen; it's impossible to predict the future in a place where you don't understand the language and where the body lingo is different. We go through several doors that remain open until we reach a locked office. In between many words I don't understand, he repeats the word triptik several times.

"Triptik triptik. Triptik triptik triptik. Triptik!"

"Triptik?" I repeat with opened arms.

"Triptik, triptik, car triptik" he insists.

I have no idea what he's asking for. I only have the European-friendly part of the insurance (it says so right on the cover) but he wants one in Turkish. Other policemen with karakolu insignias who also don't speak English arrive. They only repeat the word *triptik*.

"Triptik triptik, triptik. Triptik triptik."

"I have no idea what triptik is. Ask another driver for it. Other driver triptik. I have this, this, insurance, good – I show them the green insurance card along with my toothiest smile.

The policemen look at one another. They study the inoffensive green paper, written in a foreign language. It could be the international guarantee for a washing machine, it could be anything. Then they announce that this, what I call insurance, is invalid. Between all of them they explain that sadly all the conventions of the green card expired at the end of July, less than a month ago. *Unfortunately. What bad luck. We're very sorry.*

They want money, money to fix the wrinkle in the car, money so they don't have to fill in a bunch of forms which they would rather not do and don't fully understand. How do you process an accident where one of the vehicles and insurance are foreign? It's too complicated.

"No, no money. Insurance. I pay my insurance every month, and it's expensive, *no me jodas con eso.* Insurance okay. Green card okay. No money my friend. Insurance my friend. This is good," I affirm while continuing to smile.

In some perverse way they are charmed by the fact I'm not accepting their insinuations. They know that we're heading to Africa, they have my passport, the van's registration, my insurance and my cooperation.

I have no intention of giving them anything else. I'm hoping not to give them anything else. The reality is, however, that I can't leave unless they give me back my documents.

Or they can lock me up.

While I wait, more policemen with the same moustache approach to shake my hand. I guess crashes with foreigners are not too common.

Despite my doubts, I continue smiling. Smiling is very important. It converts you into someone closer, an innocent, a person who doesn't want problems, an idiot or a madman. The man I have bumped into looks at me incredulously with feelings that waver between curiosity and sadness. It's a bad omen to crash against a Spaniard when tonight there's a European Championship match between Besiktas and Football Club Barcelona.

"You have to pay a fine," says a King-Kong-sized policeman wearing a leather jacket. "It will be eight million five hundred thousand Turkish liras."

"What for?" Why don't you go out on the road and start fining buses and trucks that drive like suicidal maniacs, like those that two years ago caused an accident with thirty deaths in Beliçe?

The policeman looks at me with curiosity. I don't think they've ever heard of Beliçe. I do believe they are enjoying this.

"If the other driver pays the fine and I see him pay it, I will pay it too," I say in my rustic Turkish, punctuated with the body language of collisions expressed with hands that bump and fly through the air leaving many dead fingers. But most importantly, brimming with smiles. I'm saying no, yet I'm saying it with a smile.

Five minutes later the first policeman appears with his report of the accident. The famous *triptik* in Turkish. I don't understand a thing, but he tells me to sign. Then he returns my documents.

"Finish, go, you have to leave," this is the important thing: I'm not a prisoner, I don't have to pay anything.

I leave the police station without my copy of the report, *you don't need it, it's in Turkish and you don't understand a word.* We look for Fener, our cable to the earth. He's a short, thin mechanic we met when we needed to change the engine oil before the Earth accelerated. Fener has a sad smile that never really finishes, though his eyes give him away.

"Yarin" he says after checking out the bull guard, a bit loose after the crash.

"Tomorrow," he repeats.

For now, he just wants us to accept his invitation to sleep in his house.

★

At seven in the morning breakfast is served: tea, olives, scrambled eggs with tomatoes, honey, cheese, bread and marmalade. It's the first time since Switzerland that I have slept in a real bed and all my bones are aching.

Fener is pleased, the Besiktas soccer team won the match 3-0 against F.C. Barcelona and he has us on hand so he can remind us of it every five minutes. Last night the three of us sat down around a television without an image, it only transmitted the audio, excited incomprehensible voices in Turkish. Three nil is the only thing I understood and I have no other alternative but to believe him. On route to his shop we stop by a gas station to fill up with *uçuz mazot*.

"It's really bad; it comes from Russia, it's not from Iraq. It's going to ruin your engine," affirms the man in charge, who seems to be more worried about the health of our van than we are. "No, I'm sorry but I'm not going to sell it to you."

Sometimes I fondly remember that age when I lived in a predictable world. I knew the rules, I knew what to expect and what to demand from the society which surrounded me. I believed I was in a world that was continuously changing, but I was only a more or less eccentric pawn in a board marked by common places. It was the security of routine. Always the same steps, the same expressions hardly ever con-taminated with the slightest unusual tension, a tension that suggests this movement can fail and result in today's affairs being different from yesterday's.

In that world gas stations have reliable gas; the police are impartial and the judge is just; a friend opens his door and gives you a hug; you accelerate to get past the next light that will change in three…two…one second; you know that you are unlikely to be assaulted.

In the world that I knew I had insurance on almost everything. Home insurance, life insurance, insurance against work accidents paid for by the company and unemployment insurance which was deducted directly from my pay cheque; total risk coverage for the vehicle, medical insurance for my holiday out of the country and another that protected me at home when my belly hurt. There was also dental insurance, theft insurance, credit insurance, horse insurance, greenhouse insurance, insurance to protect the legs of soccer players and even against dog bites, but at the time I didn't need these. In the world that I knew only revolutions and Martian attacks could leave us destitute.

Out here habits, laws, and the use of power are different. Nothing is predictable. When we leave Turkey the last string which unites us to our old life will be broken: the insurance card is invalid in Syria.

Kemel, a long-distance bus driver, a regular at the work shop and fervent advocate of brute force, wants to straighten the van's bumper by pulling it with his bare hands. He laughs when I stop him for fear of breaking something else. A neighbour proposes that he bring his car, tie

Desolate mountains in the north of Turkey, north-east of Kurdistan.

a rope to the bumper, and speed away. Fener's friends have a dangerous tendency towards easy laughs and cheap thrills.

Fener continues working, oblivious to the rest of the world. He turns screws at his whim, first to one side, then the other, then he starts again. His helper, the Smoking Man, dedicates himself to drawing with his fingers on the camouflage of dust that covers the van. First he draws cars, then possible maps. Finally, in large letters he writes ARJENTIN + ISBANIA. Anna draws near and adds + TURKIYE.

The journey has started.

Around midday we leave towards the border with Armenia. We pass an overloaded truck heading north with bales of hay. On the side of the road hawks show off their abilities extending their wings to fly from rock to rock, and the small Kurdish villages, poor but all with satellite television, are clones of some past age. We're looking for the walled ruins of an ancient capital that was once as important and sumptuous as Istanbul. The ancient city of Ani, empty, deserted and twice betrayed, no longer exists.

The first abandonment occurred some 700 years ago due to the devastating advance of the Mongols; the second was during the Cold War, when the Soviets imposed an absolute void on all Turkish lands closer than one kilometre from the border. Nobody could work these fields, not even walk on them. It was Turkish soil, Kurdish soil, but more than anything else, it was no man's land.

An hour later some recently finished enormous white walls pop up on the horizon. Behind us a camouflaged truck arrives with some soldiers who jump out of the back and deploy at a breathless trot. The official looks around, we're still in Kurdistan. Later he approaches and orders us in French to park ten metres further away, so our van is visible from the door. He looks at the digital camera which I have in my hand and puts on an ill-humoured grimace.

"Video?"

"Oui, video et photo."

"Do you have another camera? You can't record videos inside."

I point to the sign in English which says photos and video are allowed, though it does recommend not to point towards the Armenian border.

"That is old. That stopped being in effect in July."

It appears that every written rule, every accord, expired in July. Then I ask him to look at the camera. I push a button, take out the video tape and prepare myself to lie a bit.

"I need to go in with the camera. I'm a reporter and I have to take photographs to send to Spain over the Internet. If I'm not allowed to record videos, I will leave the video tape here.

He quickly changes his expression. *Gazetecilik,* reporter, it's the magical word. Abracadabra.

"You know that we had a war?"

"Certainly, one war here with the PKK and another on the other side of the border between Armenia and Azerbaijan."

"You have been there?"

"No."

"You can tell me, there's no problem."

"No, I've never been. But I know Armenia won with the help of Russia and the soldiers who guard their borders are Russian."

"That is not an independent country. Those people you see on the other side of the gorge are not Armenians. They are Russians. Elite troops will be watching you constantly once you go through this door. They usually don't fire this way, but if they see you focusing a camera in their direction, they might. And who will punish them? Nobody. The death occurred in Turkey, but you are Spanish and the shot originated in Armenia, by a Russian sniper."

This soldier is pretty convincing.

What is left of the city of Ani, after so many abandonments and sackings, is still breathtaking. The barren ground is covered with rubble, exactly the same as you might see in photographs of Hiroshima and Nagasaki the day after the BOOOOM. The only buildings that remain standing are the decayed remains of some churches, a mosque, a convent, a palace and a large ancient caravansary. These are genuine ruins, abandoned skeletons in the middle of a massacred city, bundles of bones charred by centuries of oblivion.

"Even the sky sent down its curse" affirms the keeper who guards the entrance. "When in 1957 a lightning bolt (or a Soviet bomb) split the remains of a circular chapel in two. It was the only building that remained intact."

One-half survived, the other was converted into a confusion of bits of ornamental columns and unfinished Armenian prayers.

We walk through the streets strewn with disorderly stone rubble. A Turkish soldier pops his head out from the demolished tower of a mosque towards Armenia. On the other side of the border marked by a deep looming rocky chasm that was once spanned by a medieval stone bridge, two small armed puppets look towards Turkey with their hands on their hips.

In the middle of the destruction a ghost enters through the crack of a door of a cathedral missing its dome, or with a dome painted in sky-blue and clouds. The sculptures, the floor, the baptismal fonts and even the marble altars were stolen by thieves. Every time the thin pale spectre of the old man reaches the edge of the building, he closes his eyes and raises the palms of his hands to the height of his chest to pray. He moves his lips but makes no sound.

Five minutes later he slowly retraces his steps, and evaporates.

★

Doğubeyazıt is a big frontier town situated just a few kilometres from Iran. Today the wind is blowing from the east and the dust covers the food stores and barber shops clustered along the main street. I lean my hand on a table. A thin layer of desert particles is enough to give life a worn tone, a more subdued tired look. The sacks of grain are piled up against the walls. They're used as food, they're used as seats, and they're used as barricades to protect against mice.

Wooden carts pulled by strong horses raise the echo of their hooves as they move between taxis, buses and tractors. The loud-speakers on the mosque awaken. It's the second call to prayer, it's midmorning. Most men are wearing shirts and baggy Turkish trousers and sit on bean bags or small wooden stools to smoke cigarettes or drink tea compulsively. They all wear their statutory moustache.

Women suggest generous curves below their dresses. None of them look at the world through the grill of a burka. A veil of normalcy envelops actions with a breath of uniformity. Today is just another day, another dusty day on the first foothills of Asia.

Over the low roofs, towards the north-east, rises the snowy ridge of Mount Ararat, a land forbidden to foreigners. To get near the mountain you must obtain a military permit, and for years the systematic answer has been "No".

"Why do you want to go? It's full of bandits and wild dogs, there's nothing there," assures the police. In this prelude to the desert, nobody remembers arks or apocalyptic floods.

In the market there are more than just fruits and vegetables. There are all type of shoes, clothes sold by the kilo, fabrics with impossible patterns, old books, weird lamps, loose cigarettes and mountains of tea in boxes. Above all, however, there's more dust; determined dust that wraps static old men and insists on seasoning our every food purchase. Resolute dust, decided, crunchy dust that draws innocent whirlwinds in the air before entering your nostrils to hide from that same dust.

At one stall we ask for a kilo of tomatoes and a red lettuce and the shopkeeper offers us tea. No, it's not that classic misunderstanding between people who speak different languages: the man understands that we want tomatoes, but first he offers us tea. To accept would mean spending a good part of the day sitting on a crate of onions trying to disentangle the threads of a conversation. Before finding the right excuse I already have a small glass in my hand. Then his moustached smile (Saddam tries to find redemption again) abandons us near the water melons.

A child with a worn green coat, destroyed sneakers and sewn up trousers looks at us openly. I smile at him and he suffers an attack of shyness that floods his face with blood, but he resists the impulse to run away. Other children biting into pieces of melon approach like flies stuck on an invisible glass. Saddam the Good returns and scatters them with two words and a moderated hand that moves outwards.

The grandfather of the shop in front of us would love to be on this side. He sells lilac-coloured dresses, yellow and fluorescent orange ones with chequered pockets in black and white, though people here dress in earth tones. A dark-blue western suit walks around lost, carrying a leather briefcase while the sun heats the stalls that in a couple of months will be covered in snow.

A year ago, in Zimbabwe, I bought a bracelet with the colours of that country -- green, red, yellow and black. Coincidentally they are also the Rastafarian colours, which provoked some Africans to call me *brother, ey brother.* But here those same colours mean something else.

"Bash" says a perplexed Saddam the Good while he raises my hand delicately, repeating "good good good". Later he murmurs *"Bash Kurdistan".* That bracelet is an innocent password.

Saddam the Good has many children and lives nearby, he explains with short words while he watches me with greater care. He still doesn't know what he can say without risking everything he has. His wife. His kids. His house. His place in the market. His everyday life. His liberty. What is your highest bet? What are you willing to lose for your ideals, for your dreams?

Saddam the Good was born in Doğubeyazıt, travelled to Istanbul to complete his military service and now it's been several years since he has occupied this corner of the market. He earned it with silent effort while his wife became pregnant again and again. He works with vegetables and fruits. Under his roof there will always be enough food.

But after the first few welcoming words, the complex forecast of the times turns his joy to sorrow, to rage, helplessness and other prickly feelings.

All of this because of a bracelet with the right colours.

"Doğubeyazıt is Kurdish. So is Kars and Erzurum and Sanliurfa and Van and Batman and..."

It's the imaginary line that separates Turkey from the lands claimed by the Kurds to form an independent state. Saddam the Good has opened the floodgates of frustration and now he can't stop the flow.

"In 1988 Iraq dropped bombs on Halabja and other Kurdish towns. Gas bombs, napalm that burns the skin! Thousands of men, women and children were burnt to death!"

That started an exodus of hundreds of thousands of Kurds who left Iraq and came into Turkey. With the first Gulf War the situation seemed to change. The United States needed allies and gave the Iraqi Kurds arms and financial support to combat the real Saddam Hussein, the evil one. But they also encouraged their division into tribal clans. After the war it was simple enough to start a conflict between these clans and keep them separate.

"Germany, Greece, Italy and Russia are friends of the Kurds. Turkey, the United States and Israel are not," he assures us looking for a piece of paper between the fruit crates to scribble some numbers.

"Turkey, ten thousand Kurdish prisoners. Apo..." He crosses his arms over his chest to show the Kurdish leader Abdullah Öcalan, Apo, is dead within his prison. "Talabani and Merzani bla-bla. Now they say the Kurds and the Turks are friends. There was a war here, genuine warfare, not blablabla. Thirty thousand dead Kurds and thirty thousand dead Turks. The people, both Turkish and Kurdish, the people are good," he hesitates a moment and sighs, "but that is not enough."

With a nervous gesture he scribbles out the name Apo on his piece of paper. He doesn't know whether to believe everything he's said about good intentions and friendliness, he just wants the proof of a difficult conversation to disappear. Here everyone sympathises with the PKK, everyone wants to achieve an improbable independence. I ask about dialogue, but another shopkeeper breaks his silence and affirms that if the Turks fire on them, they have to defend themselves.

Indifferent to politics, or perhaps not, the official tea seller waits for us to empty our glasses so he can fill them again. He knows that we'll try to stop him saying that we have to visit the *tuvalet*, the stench-ridden toilet of the market, the sewer of the universe. But that's our problem; he doesn't drink that much tea.

The wind takes a break. The dust takes a seat, the spirits calm themselves and the air turns a bit more transparent. A group of women that are looking for a pumpkin ask about the foreigners.

Saddam the Good, who never stops thinking, explains that kids learn Kurdish at home but all the classes in school are in Turkish. He explains that *zor spas* means thank you, tea is called *bokua*, *havol* is friends, *nosh!* is cheers! and *rushbash* means good morning. Another seller listens to us repeating these words and gives us a micro Kurdish-Turkish dictionary. The edition is a bit precarious and the pages are not in numerical order. They jump from page 40 to 110, and later from page 1 to 39.

"If police find this on me I would have a problem. You, foreigners, no problem."

Each one of them wants to tell us their common history, their dead, the Turks, the economy of the region and the eternal broken promises from Ankara.

"Loschaniwef" says another man that approaches with more tea. It's been some time since I stopped counting. *"Apfietoso"* he repeats in Turkish so that we can understand that he has just finished wishing us bon appétit in Kurdish, while he smiles with his eyes sunk into his cranium.

I extend my hand and he not only shakes it, but covers it with his left hand so the welcome is warmer. The man shows us his HADEP credential, one of the few legal Kurdish political parties, which states he's the Member of Congress for the town. He explains with pride the mayor is Kurdish, just as in Sanliurfa and Van. I had already lost count of the military encampments and check points we had crossed easily because of our European passports.

Then he chases out the children that surround us again and raises his trouser leg to show his swollen ankle, a souvenir from his time in jail. His skin, converted into a black lump the size of a grapefruit, hides his bones. The children are still children even though they clean up the tables at the bar or carry fruit in an old wheelbarrow. The children have ears.

The man affirms that now everything is quiet. But when I ask him about the future, his hand forms the shape of a gun.

★

Before nightfall we go to an improvised campground next to the Isak Pasha Sarayii, an 18th century palace which has been recently rebuilt. From here the summit of Mt. Ararat is not visible, but the flat land below, sewn with the yellow lights of Doğubeyazıt, becomes a magical board game. These are the last days of summer, it's still not cold and a fire plays at our feet while we carbonise some potatoes.

We have dinner with a couple of fastidiously clean Frenchmen, almost out of place, who are touring around the Mediterranean in a Renault Clio. With us, beside the campfire, are two thin Iranian Kurds. One of them is named Ahmed and he's a happy man.

He's going to be married in twenty days and he's insufferably euphoric, he doesn't stop talking and blessing Allah. The light from the flames reflects in his brilliant eyes, and his mouth, enormous, stretches to hold up a smile which threatens to cut it open. He puts his hand in his pocket and pulls out a wrinkled calendar. He's a prisoner who crosses off the days to his liberty. His hand trembles in an imperceptible spasm as he raises it up to show me. Every moment that passes is one second less. But the wrinkled calendar has something odd -- the numbers.

"Farsi," explains Ahmed. "These are the numbers we use in our country."

The only ones which are similar to western numbers are the 1 and the 9. The rest are different. Zero is just a dot, 5 is an upside down heart, 6 looks like a 7, 7 is a "V," and 8 is also a "V" but inverted.

"She's 17 years old and I'm 28. I can't wait till our wedding day!" he repeats. "I studied geography and came to visit my brother because I need money. I have to pay 1,000 dollars to her father, but my good brother is going to help me."

He sweats with childish joy while his eyes open with excitement. At our feet the fire revives itself and causes the explosion of an eggplant. I move the hot coals with a stick till the flame disappears, until calm is restored.

"You know, in Iran you can't walk down the street with a girl," continues Ahmed. "The police can ask you about her and, if you are not married or engaged, you can end up in prison. The police are very, very strict in my country," he explains, referring to the Iranian Revolutionary Guard.

"And you?"

"We're engaged, there's no problem."

"But do you have some document, perhaps a letter from her mother that certifies this?"

"No, but the police only ask me her name, how old she is, the dates that already appear on her documents. If something does not coincide, you have problems. Jail. We can walk, go to the movies together, sit in the park and have an ice-cream. I can no longer establish relations with any other woman. I don't even want to. I just want her!

"And how did you meet?"

"We have known each other forever!" he responds enthusiastically. "She's my cousin!"

★

Orhan and Güzel have seven children. They live in Doğubeyazıt, on the exact border between the city and the countryside, after their home there are only cultivated fields or pastures or wild dogs or rocks or nothing. The house has an earthy smell, it's modest and has four rooms: the kitchen, a small bathroom with faucets and plastic basins to bathe, the bedroom for the male children, and the living room, which at night serves as a bedroom for the parents and their daughters. The toilet is a small wooden hut over a black pit in the garden.

We ask them directions towards Lake Van and they invite us into their home. That's the problem with this country, people never let you leave.

We take our boots off at the door and, between silences and hidden smiles, appears Nevshihan, the eldest daughter. She brings a large plastic basin filled with water so we can wash our hands and feet before entering their home. We walk barefoot on the rugs of the living room and sit on the floor, amid huge pillows, an electric tea kettle decorated with arabesques lifted from 'A Thousand and One Nights' and a Korean TV set.

When they turn the TV on it's already tuned to the international Kurdish channel. The satellite dishes which multiply over the rooftops allow the reception of the local TV channels which are broadcast from Belgium. The evening news starts in Kurdish and an hour later repeats in Turkish. The news are not good: the army has bombarded positions held by the PKK some 150 kilometres from here, near the Iraqi border. The number of dead is still unknown.

One hundred fifty kilometres is a bit more than an hour away if you have a good road next to your house.

In a corner, far from the news of the fighting, Nevshihan does her younger brother's homework. Her efforts in trying to concentrate amid all the noise of war makes her invisible. Nobody notices her. She blends into the tawdry rose-coloured wall with a fracture that rises to the wooden roof, in front of the mirrored portrait of the Prophet Ali. She disappears, autistic by vocation, to concentrate on completing phrases, doing summations or conjugating verbs in a blank workbook, her brother's workbook. She left school when she was 12 years old because she was already too old to walk the streets alone.

A picture of a demonstration hangs on the wall and is reminiscent of another fracture, young and old with their faces covered by Palestinian scarves. They are the symbols of the daily conflict. The bombings, people do not drop dead at your doorstep, but death is always near.

A little while later Orhan's brother Mehmet arrives. He lives in the house next door and his wife will be having a baby soon. He has five children who play with their cousins on the rug. Three of them are cross-eyed.

"They were born that way. It was the will of Allah."

"But can't they be operated for that?"

"Yes, but every visit to the doctor costs 20 million liras and it would require many visits. It's a lot of money. We can't pay it."

"What about at a public hospital?"

"There are no public hospitals. People get used to living with their pain until they are cured. Or they die."

"Bubli," insists Orhan, worried, "and in Brazil, how are things?"

For some historical reason neither Turks nor Kurds pronounce the letter "p". Up to this point I was Bablo, but for him I'm Bubli.

"Argentina, Orhan, I was born in Argentina, but my home is in Spain."

"Right…yes… in Germany there are many Kurds, as well as in Italy and Yunnan. Did you see how many came out on the streets when they captured Apo? And you, did you go out to demonstrate?"

The question is unexpected. It's true the capture of Ocalan in Kenya and his clandestine transfer saddened me. My impression of Turkey was of a nation that had exterminated a million Armenians 100 years ago. The Turks have never had good publicity.

Fortunately Güzel appears with dinner. She brings an enormous tray, two metre wide, packed with plates of chicken, rice, salads, radishes, cheese, and eight enormous home-made flat breads -- giant Mexican tortillas made in Kurdistan.

When we're finished, Orhan brings out his photo album. Almost all of the photos have the names of his friends written on them. We must remember, even if it involves graffiti written in pen. There he is, young and boastful, weighing fewer kilograms and with the wry face of those who still believe they are immortal. Old posed photographs in front of a wall, a rock band of the 80s, on any street, in any city of the world, but without the make-up. Boys are hugging their girls, though these ones are wearing chadors.

Later there are happy enterprising pictures of him with Güzel and their first three children in front of their new house. I compare the picture with reality, Orhan seems to confirm an old mathematical rule: the quantity of hair men have on their heads is inversely proportionate to the quantity of children they have. Two, three, five, his personal story confirms it. To date he has had seven children, and he's almost bald.

At the end of the photo album he keeps the oldest photograph, the most precious. Orhan is 14 years old and strikes a serious pose, with the exaggerated wrinkling frown that youngsters adopt when they take on the problems of adults. He's wearing an impeccable dark suit, white shirt, grey tie and worn shoes. At his side there's a little girl dressed like a woman, she holds his arm.

"This is my wedding picture."

Therefore, if he's thirty-eight and she's thirty-four, she was only ten years old when they married. It was a game.

Mehmet pulls out his photos of his military service in Malatya. In Turkey no one does his army duty in his own area: they send them to the other end of the country to avoid a group of young Kurds taking control of a battalion of tanks and planes in the middle of Kurdistan and retiring their captain with a shot to the head.

"He's been in jail for 13 years," he says pointing a finger at a taciturn youth who appears at his side. Since he was 17 years old in fact, and yet another reason for the grey hair or the lack of hair, the wrinkles, the premature aging.

Kurdish youths, Dogubeyazit, 1988

When we finish showing our photographs and explaining our history, Biribon, the little year-and-a-half-old girl, is sleeping on the carpets. Her breathing doesn't change when her father lifts her up gently with his enormous course hands. Those hard calluses are used to ploughing the land, parting water melons and lifting babies.

On the way to the toilet, outside the house, while transiting the darkness of the night, a tied-up dog does hair-raising lunges trying to reach my legs. He never tires, he knows that some day the rope will break and he will be free to bite whoever he wants. I have hardly positioned myself in front of the bowl to relieve myself of the day's tea when a voyeur appears. A small mouse, charmed by the visit, stands on his hind legs to keep me company.

Inside the house, weariness wins over curiosity. Today is a different day, but tomorrow we need to get up before dawn. The male children slowly retire to their room and I help Orhan stretch out six cushions on the floor of the salon. Ten minutes later I close my eyes. Anna, at my side but sleeping on another cushion, breathes deeply. Further on I can hear the murmuring of the children, the stillness of Nevishar and Güzel and Orhan clearing his throat, asking for silence.

I feel the firm base below my body that soon starts to fade away. The heavy red and white blankets are crushing me, I'm a sandwich, and a strange sensation of well-being comes over the house. Today was a good day.

Kurdistan...tea... The words blend together, *havol,* they soften, *nosh!* they dissolve, *bang bang,* and they turn into images. I jump from the highest dome of the Isak Pasha Sarayii and start flying over the yellow plains of Doğubeyazıt when suddenly two knocks resound on the door, *toc toc.*

Orhan gets up and floats above everyone like a clumsy ballet dancer. He opens the door. After some murmurs he calls to his wife with a sense of urgency.

"Güzel, Güzel! Mehmet's baby... Mehmet's baby!"

In the house next door the wife of his brother is giving birth. Güzel will be her midwife. There's no hospital, doctor or anaesthesia. There are no incubators, no obstetrics department or nurses with white aprons, no epidermal injections or loud-speakers to page Dr. Jones. There is no Dr. Jones here. There aren't any screams either, the night calmly continues.

★

Next morning the proud mother shows off her new baby covered in red blankets. She's tired, sitting on the same floor where she's given birth, with her face deformed by dark bags under her eyes. Despite this she gently rocks the small wooden cradle. Inside the crib, a thin, pale girl complains about her change of home. She's so small that you could wrap her in one of the large flat breads we had the night before for dinner. She's cross-eyed as well. She still doesn't know that she was born in Kurdistan, where death walks everyday among the living. "It's weird sharing so much intimacy in such a short time. Always sharing and leaving, sharing and leaving continuously," says Anna when we get back on the road.

And it will happen again. We'll install ourselves in hovels and houses of villages and cities which we'll transform into a home with foundations for a few days. We'll develop a feeling of belonging in many places; too many strangers will become friends, will become family and then become memories. We'll leave in order to start sharing again, in a different place.

I know I could become an absent-minded taxi-driver, a theatrical shopkeeper, a humble farmer, an antique dealer or fisherman, no, not a fisherman. I could be an office worker again, a stuttering teacher of languages, an arrogant bus driver, an obsessive treasure seeker, a lying tour guide, an interpreter, an artisan, a vicious gigolo and even the pastor of a new church. The truly difficult thing is to travel to the moon. I would learn Turkish and I'd be able to travel with Kazakhs, Uzbeks, Tatars, Yakutsk, Karakalpaks and Chuvash, some of the peoples of the former Soviet Union and Aral Sea region who speak Turkish dialects. I'd have to drop anchor, true, but how long would we be able to keep still now that we're actually moving?

We pass by Lake Van looking for the dinosaur the media has transformed into a cousin of the Loch Ness monster. There's nothing, not even a weird nephew with duck's feet. We tour the old cemetery of Ahlat chased by a tribe of children and we stop at the remnants of another abandoned caravansary on the Silk Road. We leave behind the exit which leads to the city of Batman and we stain the van with drops of sticky black tar from a recently resurfaced road. In the middle of a wind storm we reach the crest of Nemrut Dagi, the tomb of Antioch I of Commagene, a pre-Christian king whose sepulchre is surrounded by gigantic statues of his parents, the gods.

In Urfa we park in an ancient horse, mule and camel stable, below a pension. The room, with a shared bath at the end of the hall, faces the street. The shower is further along, past the patio where two wooden benches only a few centimetres high crack under the sunlight. Through the halls swarm traders, passengers and an old man who approaches with coins to ask permission to sleep in the bedroom on the terrace, the one without a door. I look at his face, punished with 80 years of life, though in fact he's only 52.

With the beginning of autumn we take the dusty road that goes to Syria by Akçakale. On the sides of the road survive mud-oven shaped houses with inscriptions carved with a knife. After that a military barricade appears.

There's activity today, they are painting the entry and exit doors of the country. The man in charge of the forgotten border is a well-fed and dressed politician who displays an enormous curiosity about our everyday lifestyle.

"And you sleep here?"

"Yes"

"And who washes your dirty clothes?"

"She washes hers and I wash mine."

He has an enormous hearty laugh; he can't imagine washing his own underwear.

"And the cooking?"

"Sometimes she cooks, sometimes I cook."

More laughter. A small group of functionaries and bored soldiers has gathered around to lament my unfortunate sexual equality.

"And Turkey? How did you enjoy it? Any problem?" asks a soldier stroking his moustache, the standard issue.

"No, not even one. Everything has gone very well. We do not like problems."

"We do," softly interrupts a policeman. "If there's no problems, we get bored."

We fill in three different forms from different authorities with the same information and we advance five metres, up to a tree planted in the middle of the road. A policeman signals us to pass on one side while another policeman motions us to pass on the other. I stop until they reach an agreement and advise the Syrians they're sending them a gift. The painter abandons his brush loaded with white paint and moves away from the door with a malicious smile.

FIND ALL THE PHOTOGRAPHS FOR THIS CHAPTER AT
WWW.VIAJEROS4X4X4.COM

TREADING ON HELL'S GARDEN

Only the ground, the sky and the scorpions remain unperturbed while we go through the half-opened door to Arab countries. Be careful, be careful, repeats my memory. Whenever you hear news of this corner of the planet it's because there's been a new massacre. In Palestine there's an Intifada with sticks, stones, and home-made rockets. Israel responds with aerial bombings and sub-machine gunfire. In the Hamas encampments of Lebanon, bombs take off and land like commercial jetliners at an airport. The only thing missing is the duty-free. In Iraq they're so used to violence that when a chance for peace arrives, they don't know how to react to it. Syria, the border which we have just

Photo: Caretaker at the archaeological site of Dura Europos, Syria, with his old Spanish rifle.

crossed, is the veritable House of Satan according to Uncle Sam. However, I'm not certain, I still haven't noticed the smell of sulphur.

The malicious guy who is painting the entrance to Turkey looks only at Anna. I'm not here, I do not exist. We cross the white line, the international border drawn in the sand, and we're received by a swarm of uniformed soldiers dressed in brown, without insignias but sporting the look of someone suffering from a bout of painful constipation. Among them, a slightly taller man stands out: white skin, thin moustache and olive-green uniform. He's in charge of stamping passports and asking incisive questions.

"Where are you going?"

"To Syria."

"Why?"

"Because we'd like to visit your country... we've been told the Syrian people are very friendly and hospitable."

Silence.

"What do you have here?"

"Water, wood to start a fire, food, clothes, music, tools, toilet paper, books in Spanish..." I list off in English while I open one of the van's doors.

He looks over the bag with wood, he says something in Arabic and his assistant laughs. There are many places to look but they dedicate themselves to rummaging through what they have readily at hand. It will always be the same way. They jumble up the toiletry bag with the deodorant, our combs and our toothbrushes, the toolbox, the fanny pack with tableware, the plastic container with the pot and plates. They sniff our spices and they touch up their moustaches in the rear-view mirror. They only stop when the heavy 12 to 220 volt inverter drops out and crashes on the asphalt.

The head official, stiff and with the standard furrowed brow of someone who is accustomed to being suspicious, asks about the load we carry on the roof. The murmuring from the border intensifies in volume and while I explain that on the roof we have two tires, empty fuel canisters and some spares, he turns and leaves me talking to myself.

He walks briskly towards the border's white line. When he stops he releases a barrage of frigid words filled with scorn at a corporal who continues to point towards the Malicious Turk. I don't understand a word.

"Follow me into the office," he snarls unpleasantly when he returns. "You have to pay 140 dollars."

I'm stunned. I knew that I would have to pay some insurance but... is it really that much? This is our first distant border and I'm not sure if he wants to cheat me or if it's the truth. I'm not sure if he will ever receive the money, he will say 'thank you, welcome to Syria' and hand me a photocopy. I don't know what the police and military are like in this country. I don't know how the law works and I also don't know if I have 140 dollars on hand.

Error, I don't want to look for money here. I know that there's a hundred dollars and some change in the ashtray. Error, we have little cash on hand.

I go into the office, the official is seated behind a desk shuffling some papers.

"It comes to forty dollars for insurance and for importation duties and a hundred dollars for the vehicle. It's a diesel, right?"

"Yes?" I respond, waiting for the hit.

"Special Tax for Use of Diesel. In total, it's 140 dollars." I didn't expect this revolutionary tax so soon.

"It's a lot of money," I improvise.

Again, some shouting is heard. The official arises violently, looks through the barred window with his intense frown, again that sense of constipation; he gives a gasp of exasperation and goes outside. On one side of the office awaits a round woman dressed in black, in personal mourning, who smiles at me showing three gold teeth. In other places of the world, the delicate lace which covers part of her face would be revealing her breasts.

There's movement at the border and I'm beginning to understand. The Malicious Turk who is painting the gate is constantly crossing the line on the ground to paint the Syrian side of the gate. Then the corporal shouts that he can't cross, that he's invading the territory of the Arab Republic of Syria without permission. The Malicious Turk laughs and obeys but five minutes later he crosses the white line to paint the other side of a column. He's the reincarnation of Chaplin. The corporal shouts again and the Turks laugh again.

"If we paint only one side of the gate it's going to look ugly! White on one side and rust on the other! Beasts!" I suppose he responds while he blesses Syria with a brush loaded with paint.

In the van's ashtray there are only 109 dollars. The official treats his corporal sternly. We have traveller's cheques but I doubt they'll accept them. The official invites the Malicious Turk to paint the Syrian side. There's no more money on hand. We're out of time. A bell rings, the third round starts.

"One hundred forty dollars is a lot of money. At the Consulate they didn't tell us that we had to pay so much money to bring our vehicle into Syria. I have a Visa card and 109 dollars in cash. Do you accept traveller's cheques?"

"No. Can you change them in Turkey?"

"They don't exchange at the border."

When I was eighteen every weekend I used to play poker with my friends. The timing depended on what plans there were for that night, girl or no girl, movie, billiards. We would bet coins and when we bluffed we'd bet double, according to our rules. We used to play until sunrise, and whoever won would pay for breakfast.

"We could accept 137 dollars," he affirms, assuming this drop of three miserable dollars is significant.

"This is all I have," I say, putting the 109 dollars on the table, before the brilliant smile of the Lady of the Golden Teeth.

The official furrows his brow again. If the Special Tax for Use of Diesel in Syria is an invention, he will take the money.

He purses his lips. He lifts the handset of a black Bakelite phone. The hotline to Damascus. It's a weird situation and he needs to consult his superiors before making a decision. The Special Tax is real.

Outside, the Malicious Turk crosses the border again to give some toy dolls to the Syrian soldiers, who gratefully accept them.

When the boss hangs up the receiver he begins a series of ritualistic gestures. He takes a deep breath, he stretches himself over the back of the chair, he passes his right hand over his face in a dramatic gesture and he looks at me. He studies my face carefully. I'm standing, and I tilt my head waiting for a reply. He opens his eyes a bit wider and raises his eyebrows in a silent bet. Perhaps he awaits my apprehension, that I say something unnecessary, something inconvenient, something that hides a lie, a turbid statement. Something that turns us into more than suspicious foreigners with little cash at a forgotten border.

My stomach, in knots beneath hundreds of steaks converted into my flesh, growls empty and nervous. My face remains impassive, con- firming that I'm not here, playing poker with a Syrian military official in the middle of nowhere. The only thing you want when you get to a border is to cross it as quickly as possible, to get out of there, to escape. You don't want someone to get angry with your passport, or ask stupid questions, much less intelligent ones. You've always wanted to change countries like someone crossing a street without a light, whenever you want, wherever you want.

But the world has become complicated. Now you need a special pass authorised by the king of an office, someone who has just had a fight with his wife, who has not had good sex in a long-time, who didn't sleep well the night before, who has just had a flat tire, or who, simply, is suffering from painful constipation.

As if that wasn't enough, a few weeks ago they detained a couple of Israeli spies in Damascus. Possibly he's sensitive to this new situation. Perhaps he's under strict orders. The Mossad are good at coming up with fake stories. Two hippies on their way to the ends of the Earth. Perhaps.

A minute later he breaths again, coming back to life.

"Damascus says that you can pay forty dollars now for the insurance. You can pay the rest when you leave the country. You are lucky."

He fills out five forms with the same information and pounds his desk with four stamps. Four times five: twenty PUM-PUM.

"Welcome to Syria."

★

From the road, the scenery is a monument to defeat. The brown earth, spent, fertile in stones, stretches out in every direction towards infinity. Not even a scorched bush, not one, is capable of interrupting the slightly curved line of the horizon. That space, cut with a firm hand on a scalpel, is divided in two almost identical halves, below, uniform ochre desert, above, compact blue sky.

The void. It's the first sensation you have when you cross that rocky steppe. The air compresses, heats up, evaporates. There's nothing more than spiky uncultivated land, aggressively so, charmed by a spell that's converted every blade of grass into a grain of sand. Water has never existed. Mercury, the planet closest to the Sun, is a paradise inhabited by Bedouins. If you'd be abandoned in the middle of nowhere, you wouldn't die of thirst, you'd die of anguish, of desolation.

A few kilometres later the first houses of the village of Tall Abyad appear. We travel at twenty kilometres an hour down a road which has now turned into the main street. I've seen what's happening now before, no doubt, in the swinging strut of a Bonanza episode. I arch my arms a bit more over the steering wheel. Two strangers show up on their black beast, or perhaps a dark green beast, and the entire town comes to a standstill.

Friends stop talking and look at us. A shopkeeper leans a can of food against a counter and scratches his turban. The barber drops his razor before losing his customer and his reputation, and students dressed in brown military shirts with general's epaulettes try to figure out where we're from, but they're always wrong. Young women look at us through the corner of their eye. Older women, a bit bolder, lift their heads and point with wrinkled fingers.

There is no sound on the street, just the purring of our Japanese colt. Nothing seems more important in this *Spaghetti Eastern* than our movement under the gentle sun of October.

But today is Thursday, the banks have already closed. Tomorrow, Friday, is The Lord's Day, only the mosques are open. We won't have Syrian Pounds for a couple of days at least. I think that to get some diesel, we'll have to trust in the influence of another lord, with a toupee that would be considered old-fashioned in every corner of the world. His philosophy is not well received in Syria, but everyone likes good old George Washington.

Then I understand, I know why everyone stops their life to look at the spectacle. We're cowboys from the capitalist Wild West.

At the gas station we're surrounded by two, four, eight people that continue to multiply exponentially. The fellow in charge only speaks Arabic, though he assumes, rightly, that we're after some form of combustible. But something strange happens: the numbers on the gas pump confirm that a litre costs less than a fifth of what it costs in Turkey, only ten kilometres away as the crow flies.

For a moment I feel like Alice in Wonderland. But the landing is a bit rough: Syria is ruled by a family dictatorship and books say the walls have ears, the Information Service of the Ministry of the Interior works efficiently. I remember Orwell's 1984, and I hope I'm wrong.

★

When in 1999 the water of the Euphrates began to rise, Mansur knew the dam the government had built would bring the great Mesopotamian river up to the door of his house. Everything that was growing on his lands would grow in greater abundance; impossible to imagine to his ancestors even if they combined several harvests. Redder tomatoes, sweeter pomegranates, bigger peppers and figs, softer cotton, more odoriferous mint, the desert was going to have a renaissance. During those days, the water level rose slowly up the side of the hills and, when it finally came to a standstill, it stopped four metres short of the shaded trellis covered in grapevines planted ten years before. It was a complete coincidence, but it looked calculated.

Then the scenery started to transform. The broken brown earth gave way to green pastures, and the jumping goats gave way to happy fish.

Aside from the birth of the lake, nothing ever happened in Aushariya. The remains of the nearest fortification were thirty kilometres away.

The ruins of a town abandoned before recorded history were always on the other side of the river. The secondary road is certainly far, at least five kilometres away. Between, the arid desert awaits the scarce rain of spring. Then the seeds carried by the winds will germinate and pastures will grow with no purpose other than changing the colour of the landscape for a couple of months.

A few metres from the edge of town a pregnant mother harvests some tufts of cotton off the side of a cultivated slope. Her two young boys entertain themselves making monkey faces while running and keeping an eye on the sheep so they don't get lost. Her daughters, lovely, with olive skin and green or blue eyes, clothe themselves with the most enchanting smiles as we approach. They would be fourteen and seventeen years old and in a short time someone will claim them in matrimony.

A thin tall man, with a black moustache and a clear face, appears from behind a rock. He has doubts, but he watches us gangling from behind his clear eyeglasses with golden frames. Arabs do not understand the anxiety of solitude, the silent and static contemplation of a barren wasteland. They approach, they sit down and talk, or they gather near in an uncomfortable silence. Nothing is more annoying than a vacuum. Here they take the proverb "hell is where there are no people" very seriously.

"Isbanya-arab brothirs," he says after discovering our origins only thirty seconds after losing control of his legs which inevitably drag him towards the van. *"Al-Andalus Magreb,"* he repeats while he enmeshes the fingers of his hands to underline a common past.

I nod and smile while he regains his confidence in his stumbling English. His uncle, silver haired and as wide as a kitchen drawer, approaches with a bag full of fish still trying to breathe water, and offers us tea. Within five minutes there's fish, and lamb and chicken, and he wants us to follow him to his house. They're Syrians, but they're also Countryside Arabs, so they have an uncontrollable urge to be hospitable with the strangers they find wandering through their lands.

The Man Who Lost Control of His Legs is named Nouraddin and is thirty years old. He's the second son of another big family and thus, perhaps because of his large and skeleton-like stature, or to a carefully calculated family ambition, he hasn't followed in his brother's footsteps by joining the Syrian army. He studied to become a lawyer. His father, strong and vigorous, is a farmer and has a Hollywood style Arab name: Mansur. His mother, who follows, is named Ferithe. Further back appear brothers and sisters who no one bothers to introduce. Or perhaps they're too young or they're girls who have reached that dangerous age when men start looking at them like women.

"And the two of you, are you married?" asks Nouraddin. It seems important.

Yes or no. In Arab culture there are no shades of grey. The attitude of 'we're giving it a try' or 'we're getting to know each other' does not go over well. It's either yes or no. The wedding determines the respectability of the guests. Thus we always say "yes": the opposite could be interpreted to mean that Anna is still available, even though we live together. Then Ferithe gets involved.

"My mother wants to know if your families arranged the wedding and what the conditions were," translates Nouraddin.

Tricky. I knew Anna's family just a few months before we departed; they wanted to know who was kidnapping her. One falls in love with another person, but behind them is their mother, their father, their cousins, uncles, grandfathers, nephews and worst of all, their friends. You have to be liked by them, else you are newly screwed. So that was how I, who had always been careful with my words, found myself suddenly married, with a ring as big as a 4x4 van.

Ferithe smiles and nods when Anna explains that we're together because we want to be.

In Arab countries, land, sheep and women are combined in the same rights of property overseen by the male head of the family. I make a few calculations; Ferithe must have married Mansur when she was twelve to fourteen years old, probably as an imposition she accepted as one of the unavoidable rules of life. With the birth of their children she learned to love him, though it surprises me that she struggles away from his embrace with annoyance when I take their photograph.

Mansur's family. The man at the right of the photo is Nouraddin.

"This coming year, *inshallah,* my father will find a second wife," affirms Nouraddin. "My mother doesn't like this." In Syria men can have up to four wives according to law, but they have to maintain them and treat them as equals.

"And women, are they allowed to have up to four husbands?" I ask amusedly.

"No! If a woman sleeps with another man who is not her husband she would be shunned and isolated by the entire town! She would be dirty!"

At the age of sixty Mansur wants a second wife. Ferithe can no longer give him children. Though we say she looks strong, he assures us that she's old. His body calls for war, pitched battles, outbreaks, fresh meat, and he knows that in town he can get whichever bride he wants. He's a serious man, a land owner, he sells his cotton to the government and he finds himself in an unbeatable position to negotiate for a new wife.

I look at his daughters, who submissively bring tea and submissively retire. Matrimony appears to be a bureaucratic process, an economic accord between families for arranged procreation, an assembly line for the production of children.

★

Before midday the men start arriving. A grey-haired colonel who will shortly be promoted brings the eldest son from Damascus, Mansur's military son.

"It's 455 kilometres and we've arrived in little more than two hours. With my new Mercedes Benz I can reach speeds up 230 kilometres an hour," assures the colonel, enjoying the sound of his words before reclining lasciviously on the cushions which surround the garden in front of the Euphrates.

Another friend of the family arrives from Mambj, some forty kilometres away. He's in charge of the water supply and distribution in the region, an important job when you live in the desert. He's about fifty years old and dyes his hair youthfully black. His face points downwards, sharpened by a big nose and a constant smile, without molars.

At my side is seated an older man, I would bet the van that he's involved with the intelligence services. For quite a while he silently watches us. His attentive eyes framed with fine but bushy eyebrows stare at us.

He must be reading our minds. Israeli spies have certain tics which Arabs do not have. For example, sometimes they'll let out a shalom, or they have their hair plastered on the crown of their head, the mark of a yarmulke. I smile. Finally, he presents himself as an old professor of English who lives in Aleppo. Sure.

"You have green eyes, like the Arabs," he later says.

"Must be because of Al-Andalus," I proclaim. "My grandfather's, grandfather's, grandfather was surely an Arab."

This is how I gained a place in Muslim paradise; surrounded by fruit trees, crystalline streams and seventy-two houri, seventy-two spiritual virgins, seventy-two Virgin Mary's capable of conceiving while still maintaining an irrational purity. Seventy-two perfect women, mothers and wives, flying around me all day.

Hmmmmmmm...

From then on everything unfolds calmly. The food is Babylonian, prepared for ten mouths seated in front of a giant plastic tablecloth five metres long. The trays arrive from the kitchen brimming with plates of fried fish, salads, baked lamb, tenderloin fried in onion juice, spiced rice, small pieces of chicken, peppers in vinegar, home-made sauces, freshly baked bread right out of the oven, and pan-fried peppers. Everything is in exaggerated quantities that supersede the capacity of our stomachs. This is opulence; a stage production of well-being. That's when I remember the leftovers are to feed the women and children of the house.

Anna is the only female accepted permanently at the table, she's a foreigner. Ferithe calls on her years as matriarch, and without anyone opposing accommodates herself next to her military son. She hardly touches the food. Now that he's home she prefers to caress his hair.

A short while later, Uncle Fisherman and a servant with three teeth replace the half-empty plates with others containing fruit. Tea and coffee arrive soon afterwards and the afternoon continues with the monotonous drone of a distant water pump. The conversation drifts towards politics, which means Israel must be renounced.

"Nothing remains of the French occupation," recounts Professor of English. "Few people speak French; the borders they imposed on the country have only served to separate families because they are not real. They are just straight lines drawn by colonial bureaucrats who intended to divide Greater Persia into four countries: Iraq, Syria, Lebanon and Jordan. It was an effective way of weakening us."

When we declare ourselves to be satisfied and, *hamdulillah,* we praise Allah; Uncle Fisherman and the Servant with Three Teeth gather the plates. Mansur knows that if his daughters showed as much as the tip of their noses, they would run the risk of becoming the dessert of these old foxes. He would do the same.

The eldest would be about sixteen and her severe look is focused on the cement floor. An ancestral anger against the world permeates her every move. She never smiles. When she leaves the kitchen she walks towards her objective with precise steps, without wasting any time on useless diversions, without frivolous detours, without distractions. She seems to have been educated firmly. Her sister is about fourteen years old, and the rigours of a life devoted to housework have not yet extinguished the look of curiosity from her eyes. She can't help smiling and looking at us with furtive glances or directly when the adults are not around.

From a Western perspective, it's difficult being a woman among traditional Arabs. Her life is limited to being under the strict supervision of her father and afterwards her husband. Her studies, especially outside major urban centres, finish abruptly when she's eleven to thirteen years old and she awakens in a bed stained with blood, such as what occurred to Nevshihan from Doğubeyazıt. Starting with the first menstruation, little girls become exclusive assistants to their mothers. Her university will be the house; her homework will be the kitchen, washing cloths and cleaning rugs, sewing, manners, respect and obedience. She will need to cover her hair with a scarf, a *hegab*. Her arms and legs will remain hidden. Once she is married off her husband will decide what clothes she must wear. Perhaps he will let her keep her head uncovered; perhaps she can wear a *chador* which will only hide her hair and her neck. Or perhaps he will only let her eyes be seen. Perhaps he'll insist she covers herself completely, and look at the world through the grill of a *burka* and wear gloves to hide her nails. It's possible that she may be required to share her husband with other women.

From the perspective of a traditional Arab, it's easy to be a woman within Islam. Her life is removed from the concerns and dangers of the world, since first her father, and then her husband are there to protect her. Her future is assured at home, caring for her children and ensuring that happiness reigns under her roof. That's why it's important to know how to cook well, how to manage a home, and learn to obey and respect her father and husband. Men, who are strong, are responsible for all exterior problems, from dressing her to feeding her properly. He's in charge of making the money and managing it well so she can have a happy life.

A happy life.

★

As dinner time approaches, guests start to arrive again. The fellow in charge of water distribution joins our all-inclusive accommodation. A brother of Ferithe and a man dressed like a policeman have heard that at Mansur's house there are a couple of foreigners. They also show up.

"My uncle," says Nouraddin when the policeman extends his cold, slippery hand, like a fish just out of the water. It's unpleasant.

Uncle Policeman has weird gestures. He rarely speaks and almost always turns his head rapidly and suddenly, as if he were waiting to discover something hidden, a concealed sign, a complex wink, a shared ultra-secret codified language with Anna. Nouraddin also acts strangely. Every time we discuss something in Spanish he shouts "What?" as if he had not understood something.

His sisters have disappeared again. They're never around when we have breakfast, lunch or dinner; the dishes are their presence.

This time we meet in the small lounge room that we use as a bedroom. The four walls are surrounded by white curtains embroidered with aquatic plants, flowers and ducks, and the ceiling is made of woven straw matting supported by four beams. Arab tradition requires that if a guest shows interest in something, the host must give it to them. Thus the room only has drapes.

The dinner is abundant and quiet. Sitting on the floor, amid all the dishes, nobody says a word. Only a couple of unpleasant sounds occur, plates, glasses, and the rhythmic chewing of Uncle Policeman. Open mouth, close mouth, open mouth, close mouth. We're the invited guests; therefore the Water Manager offers us the most desired portion of the dish: the steaming brain of a lamb served in its skull which has just been split open by hand.

I never refuse to try new dishes. However, when he explains that I should plunge my hands into that mass of happy memories of pasture and wanderings in the desert, times of plenty or draught and fleeting amorous encounters on the grass, *baa-baa,* I simply can't. I have eaten some truly disgusting things: worms, termites and scorpions, questionable stews in seedy bars, skewered meat that likely belonged to a stray alley cat during some local festival, possible some missing neighbour that ended up in a stew in some remote village.

But I can't do this. I politely refuse the privilege; I'm just not prepared for it today. The look on the face of the Water Manager reflects his disappointment, though, it's a feigned disappointment, because seconds later he leans the hollowed out bone on the metal tray. It must be a delicacy.

"Have you ever had problems with your passports while crossing borders?" asks Nouraddin.

"No, never."

"You must have stamps from many places... Can I see them?"

After looking at my passport page by page he asks me for Anna's. When I pass it to him, he gives it directly to Uncle Policeman, who's just visiting.

"I'm showing it to him because he will give you some advice," he responds when I look at him with surprise.

Uncle Policeman reviews the passports page by page paying special attention to the expired visa stamps from Egypt. His dedication surprises me.

"What about the papers for the van? Do you have them here?" asks Nouraddin.

Something is starting to smell bad and it's not the lamb's brains. The anxiety which Uncle Policeman exhibits with regards to our passports is starting to become annoying.

He's probably looking for proof which betrays the fact that we have passed through Israel. Stamps from the Egyptian or Jordanian border at Eilat or Jerusalem are enough grounds for immediate expulsion from the country. Foreigners that have stepped on Israeli soil are not welcome in Syria, Iran or Sudan. Such is the collateral damage from religious wars.

Then he unexpectedly remarks on a different stamp.

"Bolivia!"

Uncle Policeman's visit is not casual; our host advised him that he had two foreigners in his house. He invited him to come over for dinner. He gave us shelter, like a good Muslim and, being a good Syrian, informed the authorities of any abnormal event. We are certainly abnormal. He would find some excuse to examine our passports. You never know after what happened with those Israeli spies captured in Damascus. Foreigners never pass through Aushariya so perhaps we have entered the country illegally. He is a good citizen who works with the government of his Excellency President Bashar al-Assad, beloved son of Hafez al-Assad, may Allah smile on him. Therefore, as a lawyer, he respects the laws of his country and wants order.

When Uncle Policeman returns our passports, I give him a stupid look, directly; one of those looks which leaves no doubt. *You disgust me.* Something which should never be done but which at times is irresistible.

"Tell me, what sort of advice can Uncle Policeman give us?" I ask Nouraddin.

"What?"

"What sort of advice can your uncle, Mister Policeman, give us after examining our passports?"

"What?"

"Your curtains have ducks on them and they're very nice! I love the curtains with their duckies!"

★

The next morning, after an excessive breakfast which leaves us stuffed until dusk, Ferithe loads us up with jars of fig marmalade, apricots and grapes from their own vines, with green Syrian olive oil, very green, and bags filled with crushed sesame seeds. She smiles, she's a mother. While we fit in all the food I ask Nouraddin about the basis of Syrian law.

"It's based on Egyptian legal code and the French Constitution."

"What about the Koran?"

"The Koran only applies to women. This is intended to protect and care for them."

"And what do you, being a lawyer, think of this double standard?"

"In the villages, they're governed by tradition, in the cities it's different," he responds, after a moment of doubt.

As we leave, for the first time I touch the warm hands of his sisters. The eldest, serious and austere in her emotions, cold, remotely controlled by the influence of tradition, starts to weep in silence amidst the fruit trees of the garden.

Nouraddin then comes over and whispers a secret.

"I have a girlfriend in the city."

As we drive away, I see the whole family, gathered by the side of the road waving us goodbye as if it were the end of a fairy tale, a fable that ends with handkerchiefs waving in the air. Left behind is the conflict between hospitality and paranoia, between the Arab heart and the fear of power. Anna drives.

The eldest daughter hides her face behind her hands. Her sister slowly lowers her head. Her eyes stop shining.

My heart fills with sand.

The Muslim calendar began with the last flaming rays of the setting sun of July 15, in the year 622 of the Christian chronology, when the prophet Mohammed went into exile in Yathrib, now Medina, in the Kingdom of Saudi Arabia. When we join the chaotic traffic and the maddening misuse of horns in the streets of Aleppo, all at the same time from every direction, destroying our patience and our good-will, we're back in 1420. Changes occur through the windows at the speed of a trip through time.

"Salaam aleikum," may peace be with you, greets one of Ali Baba's companions, eager to sell us a flying carpet when we park in front of his store. The human landscape has left behind the Ottoman trousers to cover itself up with Arab galabiyas.

"Aleikum salaam," may you go in peace, replies Anna anticipating my response. It's been two hours since we left Aushariya and she has not forgotten the women.

Some steps away begins the souk; an endless succession of narrow passages invaded by a pandemonium of goods. It's a huge, dark, noisy and wrinkled maze, a high-ceilinged labyrinth where bodies move, bump and trip with sacks of grain, cardboard boxes and abandoned stools. The animals push and the yellow light bulbs that hang from thin wires unleash an apparent epidemic of hepatitis.

Every five to ten metres the air changes in consistency and a new contradiction arrives to your nostrils. Sweat, pepper, incense, sesame, sweet tobacco, cumin, urine, raw meat, smoke, donkey dung. The senses get excited, it's provocation after provocation, first spicy, then sweet, then bitter, until they all start to combine. Tea, olives, camels, green pistachios, henna, crushed tomatoes. Your antennae are unbalanced, or worse, confused.

The smell is so intense that you start to taste it; your mouth fills with thick saliva soaked with volatile particles. Bananas crushed by the hoof of a donkey taste like overripe avocados. A corner full of garbage and flies tastes like a dog's breath. It's surprising how much frothing saliva you can create to clean the palate. The dragging gait of an old man tastes like antique dust or a closed up and humid house. A blind man could navigate without needing a guide towards the corner that always smells of camel urine. Your mouth becomes contaminated.

The lateral passages take impossible curves towards blind alleys filled with shoemakers and hawkers without any defined profession. We traipse through shops specialising in genuine and fake jewellery run by gentlemen with a suspicious air of respectability. There are textiles by the yard, trousers, galabiyas for gentlemen, chadors and burkas with the latest fashion designs for women, Rolling Stone T-shirts, dried fruit, mirrored or silvered ornaments, dense olive oil and several small mosques built in the memory of forgotten holy men. To the right a carved portal opens out to an ancient *khan,* a lodging for travellers and caravans which now serves as a sewing workshop.

The ground, hard and rough, changes consistency and becomes a skating rink of effervescent life in the section dedicated to slaughtered meat. It's the nightmare of a housewife used to pristine supermarkets.

Excuse me, where are the frozen foods? A store offers beverages of all colours and flavours except Pepsi or Coke. Syria is one of few countries in the world that has shut the door to symbols of American culture.

Almost all numbers are in Farsi. The price of a kilo of mandarins is in Farsi. Public phones have buttons in Farsi. The date printed on the cover of the local paper, number plates on cars and taxis are all in Farsi. Even the visas have the entry stamp and time allowed written out in Farsi. The Farsi numbers surrounding us are reminders the scribbles we use in the West are only one of many numerical systems throughout the world.

Behind a fortress of cardboard boxes, the citadel emerges. It's the symbol of Aleppo and the scene of the most important religious wars in history: the Crusades. Islam advanced from the Arab peninsula conquering everything with the slogan 'if you do not convert, we'll have to kill you'. The Crusades fought back in order to 'exterminate the infidels and purify the Holy Land with blood'. Thus began the problems in the Middle East: God made a clerical error and sold the same Promised Land to several peoples.

The most striking thing about Aleppo is the worship and exhibition-ism of the al-Assad family, who have been in power since 1970. There are posters with the president's photo throughout the souk, in shops and public buildings, homes and lamp posts. Many vehicles windows are covered with stickers bearing the face of the late Hafez al-Assad super-imposed on the breast of an imperial eagle. Invariably he's surrounded by his sons, the current president Bashar al-Assad and his late brother Basil, wearing police eyeglasses and striking a Rambo-like pose. Their images are everywhere, framed by ornate filigree borders of coloured lights, and even decorate the bumpers of minibuses.

It's the omnipresent marketing of power, the gesture which reaffirms the fidelity of the second largest city in the country to the government in the capital. It's a confirmation of the Cult of the Blessed Trinity. The Father who is in heaven, the Son who is in government, and the Holy Spirit, the eldest son who should have been president, but instead died in a traffic accident.

The desert opens out into an infinite number of unmapped tire tracks under the bearable sun of October. Our imagination and the traces which survive the breath of wind draw us off-road, towards any of the small ridges that rise out of the horizon. The temptation is strong. The ground, gardens of course sand and rocks incrusted by the few drops of rain which fall every four or five years, gives us the freedom to travel in every direction. The landscape, seemingly empty, is full of long individual images; of lost telephone poles and men convinced that time is just an invention of complicated people. We're looking for Ibn Warden, an extravagant Byzantine castle built over a thousand years ago in the middle of nowhere, for a tough governor whose job it was to control the Bedouins, by reason or by force.

The road unwinds unencumbered by any signs that could be interpreted as a demarcation of traffic control. This is right and this is left, you go this way or that, simple, pure logic among equals. This works until you run into a truck, then your tires will raise a fine layer of dust off the pavement. Presuming the road will be split down the middle is a dangerous provocation, Russian roulette with a loaded revolver.

As we travel deeper into the desert the flies appear. One. Two. Ten. They fly into our ears; they land on any part of our skin exposed to the sun. They say that in Palmyra it's worse, there are clouds of them there. They are the omnipresent music which accompanies you while you walk amidst the columns and pomegranate trees, and fly in your mouth, your nose, and stick to your sweat. They seek out the moisture of your eyes to lay their eggs in some cosy corner. They only disappear at night when the cold makes them sink into a lethargic torpor, till the first rays of sun break over the horizon.

The radio plays Egyptian pop music. *Oh habibi, habibi...* I unfold the map of Syria. The printed names don't always match the real names of the villages, but we must be near. On the side of the road the houses are camouflaged into the sand, with brightly painted doors that make it easy to imagine climate change. Recently this area was a jungle with toucans and peacocks. Life was red, green, orange, blue, lilac and turquoise, like the eyes of the bricklayer who enters the store to buy a bottle of Al-Kola. This yellow grey dust that covers everything did not exist then, the colour of the doors still lives on in some corner of the collective memory. Then something small appears on the horizon; it's a bit different from the rest, thick walls made of red and white rock. The ruins of what must have at one time been a unique castle. Ibn Warden.

We park in the shade of one of the great walls inscribed with pre-Christian religious symbols; goat's heads, spirals, chalices and squares filled with dots. A young Bedouin with blue eyes approaches. He sports a trimmed beard and he's dressed in a dark-blue galabiya beneath a leather jacket. His name is Mohammed and he invites us to the house of his uncle, the Castle Warden. On the door a sign still reads 'Maison de la Mission National'.

"Not many tourists come here, there are no buses and the road finishes twenty kilometres in the sand," he explains in good English motioning his hand towards the undulating soft ground that extends the same here as it extends over there.

Bedouin means nomadic desert dweller. For thousands of years they were the owners of this terrible land, the empty spaces between Syria, Jordan and Iraq. This place was the prelude to death, a blindingly sunlit place that provoked madness and swallowed entire caravans without leaving a trace. The most logical saw their sanity run ragged until it lay in tatters. Their abilities as warriors and bandits without scruples were only comparable to their instincts of being able to stay alive from oasis to oasis. This is how they occupied the most ferocious deserts, the Najd and the Hadramaout in the Arabian Peninsula, the North African Sahara. The empty spaces on maps.

Today, just as a thousand years ago, they still survive on a diet of rice, flour, camel milk and crispy roasted goat coated with sand. They know the harshness of the desert, which is why they welcome newcomers with open arms.

We leave our boots in the interior patio, facing the doorway to the salon, and we sit on cushions spread along the perimeter of the wall without showing the soles of our feet. That would be an insult. A pair of woman's hands covered in henna drawings leaves a tray at the door. Bitter coffee flavoured with cardamom; genuine Bedouin *qahwah saadah* which occupies not more than a centimetre in the small earthenware bowls. I drink it and give the empty cup back, but Mohammed fills it again, tilting his head slightly.

"Thanks, that's enough."

"Then you must return the cup like the Bedouins, moving your wrist from side to side. Have another coffee."

After doing it right, Mohammed smiles and offers the cup to Anna. When the coffee ceremony has finished the ceremony of questions begins.

"Are you married? Do you have children? Are you one of those who make the sign of the cross? What is your house like? Do you have pictures? What do you do for a living? How much do you make? Do you have a big family? Are your parents alive? How much did your van cost?"

Each response is translated for Uncle Castle Warden who has just entered and said "no English," and smiles every time we say something in Arabic, "little Arabic."

"Here, we know one another. The reality is that we're all from the same family, uncles, cousins, brothers..."

In the desert, land is free and villages grow as children have more children and they marry their cousins or marry women from the neighbouring village, some eight kilometres away, who are all from the same family as well.

The hands of his invisible wife leave another tray, this time with tea. A child pops his head around the corner and Mohammed starts preparing a narghile, a hookah.

"Have you seen any eagles?" he asks holding the fragrant tobacco, moist and sticky, strawberry flavoured, which stains the hard tips of his fingers with a reddish tinge.

"Only a few. We saw more of them in Cappadocia and in Kurdish Turkey."

He becomes still for a moment and considers Anna's words. He places the stack of tobacco on top of the narghile and repeats the action a couple of times. Then he covers it with metal foil and pierces the top with a pin.

"Would you like see one?"

We cross the white patio and we stop in front of the grilled window of a bedroom. Inside, a peregrine falcon stands upright on the back of a chair.

"I use it for hunting. I purchased it in England, where they're trained. You have to go there a couple of times to choose an animal and so that they get used to your voice. They teach them two or three words, one to go and another to return. They cost about 5,000 dollars. It's a good animal."

When we return, he stands the water pipe in the middle of the room in front of his bent knees. He takes a bare dried corncob and places it on a burner that makes it glow red hot. Then he lifts it with some rusty tongs and puts it over the tinfoil. He slowly begins to suck the tip of the flexible tube connected to the centre of the pipe. After the first breath he exhales air, but after the second breath he puffs out a thin stream of perfumed smoke. The tobacco is now lit, and the smoke reaches the lungs as fresh strawberry-scented air.

Then Mohammed offers us the pipe from the narghile. Anna seems undecided. It does not look too hygienic, but it serves the same function as Argentinean Yerba Mate; something which is shared, and keeps the conversation going. And it tastes good, it's the closest thing to smoking a stick of bubble gum.

Uncle Castle Warden rises and brings a photograph where he poses with a hawk that scans the horizon. Between them there is a mysterious fundamental communication, a support, a tacit agreement of loyalty. The animal keeps its eyes on some distant point while Uncle Castle Warden looks at it with the love that you can only profess for an old friend.

"He was called Djana and was very good. We would go out into the desert to hunt rabbits and birds and he responded well to commands. Djana died two years ago from an infected leg which the doctor could not cure. It was a shame."

The bereavement is cut short unexpectedly by the purring of two motorcycles which approach and stop at the door.

"Gouac!" I greet in Bedu, as we go outside and the brilliant and murderous sun continues scorching the ground.

Mohammed looks at me and smiles. These are his cousins, from the next village. He approaches one of the motorcycles, takes a plastic bottle attached to the handlebars and pulls out a dove dressed in a small leather jacket. It could be a beautiful Hell's Angel, but no, "the jacket is so the eagle can catch the dove in mid-air without hurting it." This way it will only suffer a heart attack.

The other motorcycle has a sparrow that is trying to escape. He slinks, opens his wings with desperation, extending his neck to the sky, towards independence. But his flight is cut short and he falls to the ground with surprise, where he flaps and stirs with rebellion or terror. He has a string tied to his leg which is tied to the motorcycle.

The cousin looks at him calmly; he knows he won't go far. His freedom measures two metres.

Abu Saif was born in Saudi Arabia thirty-eight years ago. He's dressed in dark-blue trousers, a striped shirt, shiny black shoes and the smug smile of a well-paid businessman who shows his wealth without scruples. He has a thick and perfectly trimmed moustache and his languid gaze matches a certain corpulence which tends towards fatness. He has an enviable aura of satisfaction. His whole being exudes an air of success and progress, the natural magnetism which emanates unconsciously from the select few. We met him in a street in Deir ez Zor, a crossroads a bit more than 100 kilometres from the Iraq border, when he offered us the "unique opportunity to taste the best falafel in the entire Middle East."

His place of business is thin and long, with a full-length counter that divides the space in almost two equal halves. In the dimly lit recesses at the back of the shop is a very basic washroom with a squat toilet and a twenty-litre oil bucket filled with water. On the walls hang some faded mirrors and a couple of posters depicting the human tides of Mecca. We settle in on a pair of high stools and while he washes his hands he starts telling us his story. He works eight months of the year in a five-star hotel in Riyadh. The other four months he lives amid the semi-Western beaches of Lebanon, *ahhh Lebanon!*, and his small food stand in Deir ez Zor, the land of his mother.

He dries his hands with a rag and dips a dozen croquettes of mashed chickpeas and spices into the boiling oil. The crackling of the seasoned crust awakens the lethargy of the stomach with promises before noon. It's the same sound as small fireworks, the sound of fuses running to their dynamite destination. Then, though I would never have thought it possible, an extremely thin man crosses the threshold of the door and seems astonished to see me. He stands there unblinking. A long thick beard covers his face. He's wearing a turban that was once white and a worn out galabiya.

His posture changes again. His surprise gives way to tension; he looks like a crouched fighting rooster, ready to jump. Spontaneous violence is extremely rare during a trip. Sure, someone could steal a neglected purse, break a lock and rob you, but unprovoked beatings and shootings because of where you're from are pretty rare.

"American?" he asks.

In these cases, the fault is of the Americans, or the Russians, or the Chinese, or the Latin Americans, or the immigrants, or the neighbour who lives on the other side of the arbitrary border that was delineated a long time ago. *They take our jobs, or our women, or our street, or our hope of a perfect world, just as we'd like it. They ruin the look of the neighbourhood. They don't believe in what we believe. These strangers, they are responsible for our unhappiness.*

"American?" he asks again.

"No, *Spani.*"

"Ahhh, American ta-ta-ta-ta-ta-ta!" he states with unconcealed rage, squeezing the trigger of an imaginary Kalashnikov.

Then he turns around and leaves, disappearing as quickly as he came.

Despite the *ta-ta-ta,* in Deir ez Zor the atmosphere is relaxed. The political centre of the country is far away and the burkas remain in the closet. You can find a weirdo, naturally, though the odds of encountering such a character are much lower than in New York, Madrid or Buenos Aires.

We all carry a tiny sleeping Nazi in our wallets.

Near the limits of the city we meet the Euphrates again, which provides unique opportunities for recreation and relaxation such as fishing with explosives. The river is shiny and deceptive; it appears to flow gently but it's a lie. It's a giant leaking pipe that moves forward, losing volume in the sands and cultivated fields of its shores. At its delta, it no longer deserves to be called the Euphrates. It's the anti-river.

"Don't even think about it," says Anna as I watch mesmerized. "I know what you're thinking. Forget about it."

"But I didn't ..."

"Forget it".

Abu Saif getting shaved in a barbershop at Deir es Zor

But before trying new angling methods, we must pay a courtesy visit: foreigners in Syria must register every fifteen days at the police station. They confirm that you have a visa, they attest to your presence, and they control you. We are joined by Abu Saif, the best falafel chef in the world.

The city is amazing; nobody hesitates to drive in the wrong direction down a one-way street to find a short cut. When I reach a corner the traffic light turns red and I stop. On my left pass four adults sitting on a scooter, an image that should have a place of honour and glory in the annual martyrdom of Italian and Japanese bike manufacturers.

Abu Saif looks at me with surprise. "What are you doing?"

"The traffic light is red."

"Never mind. Go! Go!"

"There are two policemen over there. I don't think they will like it."

Two cars go around us blowing their horns, angry at the obstacle in the middle of the street. The policemen look at us in astonishment, one speaks to the other and motions us to advance. A hundred yards later the street turns into a one-way street and we're going in the wrong direction.

"Which way do we go?" I ask.

"Straight ahead," replies Abu Saif.

"But we're going against traffic on a one-way street."

"The signs are just decoration. Just go straight, there's no problem. If the police say something you just give them five pounds." Five Syrian pounds is less than a dollar, it's ridiculous.

Absurdly, believe it or not, Abu Saif seems to recognize all the uniformed and civilian personnel who work at the police station. He knows that to renew your visa, first you have to find such-and-such a paper, fill it out, have it stamped, have it translated into Arabic at that office, have the chief read it over and sign it, two pictures please, another signature, you're missing this information. Meanwhile we drink tea and remember the names of our mother and father. In Arab countries there's nothing like having a local helping you out with all the bureaucratic paperwork.

Half an hour later we go to his house, where he hoards a few Al Chark beers in the fridge. You have to drink them cold, extremely cold: it's like drinking bottled diesel, probably the worst beer on the planet.

We're joined by his forty-year-old brother who just remarried a young sixteen-year-old girl a few weeks ago. He is still officially married to his first wife, an Iraqi who lives in Canada with their two children.

"I married her to please my mother, who is Christian. She believes that it's not right for a man to live alone," he confesses, and shrugs his shoulders.

Abu Saif also wants to get married. He wants Anna to find him a woman in Spain; her sister Pilar, perhaps. We're just joking, until he asks what her price is, squinting his lucky little Arabic eyes.

"Women can't be bought in Spain," replies Anna.

"Marriage is not as simple as you think. It's not a commercial transaction, but rather it's emotional. In Spain the boy and the girl have to know each other, discuss, go out, fall in love or not, and in time may decide to share their lives, with or without a wedding."

Abu Saif listens attentively, trying to assimilate all this information. In his head he's doing the math: they don't cost any money but perhaps I have to stay a year in a foreign country. In Europe, that could be a lot of money, more than what several camels might cost. Nor is it a risk-free business transaction.

"Tell me something," continues Anna, "how would you like her? With a chador or without? With a burka?"

"Noooo, I want to see her face!"

"Don't you like women in bikinis?" I ask.

"Certainly, that's why I go to Beirut," he assures us, smiling a bit more. "There, women are more liberal and it's quite easy finding company."

I look at Anna and I suddenly realise that we have to hide our body language. In Arab countries it's not advisable to hold someone by the waist, no couple walks hand in hand, nobody gives or receives spontaneous kisses at the bus stop. Small nibbles on the street would be a public offence, and could constitute a crime.

Someday progress and economic development will send Islam to the corner of traditions, like what occurred in Europe with Christianity. Then there will be a sexual revolution led by educated women, tired but proud, and some hippies wearing a turban. Then there will be a real encounter between civilisations: Christians, Muslims and Jews will mingle in bed.

I take another sip of Al Chark, a shudder runs through my body. I now understand why they don't drink alcohol in Arab countries. It's vile stuff.

On TV there's a documentary about Spain and bullfighting. *"Oleeeey!"* shouts Abu Saif. Tony Manero dances on another channel. On CNN someone important from the US is asking Bashir al-Assad to stop supporting Hezbollah because it's attacking Israel. Bashir al-Assad answers that he can't stop them because he's following the will of his people and they are sympathetic to the plight of that Islamist group. Past channel one hundred there's TV from Iran, Iraq, Qatar, Saudi Arabia and Egypt.

On Al-Manar, Hezbollah's channel, a man preaches hatred against Israel amid images of Intifada, the wounded carried on shoulders, Palestinians picking up and throwing back gas grenades like baseballs and histrionic shouting women. If Europeans and Latin Americans unfetter their anger in huge soccer stadiums, here in Syria that purification ritual is actualised in the weekly protests against Israel. On screen, some men shoot into the air and women scream angrily, raising the Koran and moving about with a surprising freedom.

"Take this, so you do not forget me," says Abu Saif extending his hand when the commercials start. "If you find me a wife in Spain, let me know, okey?" He gives me a silver-plated hexagonal key chain that reads 'Saudi America'.

The desert is a succession of rocky plains betrayed by rivers and the murderous desperation of the sun. According to the map, somewhere behind these mountains which rise to the right there's another ruined fortress. But on the ground there are no signs or markers or roads or tracks or anything.

Only grey shattered rocks that lost their struggle.

We stop at a crossroads, a service station strategically located in the middle of hell, which is probably the loneliest place on Earth. There are almost decent bathrooms, a small store with basic items, and the shell of a crushed scorpion near the gas pumps. The sky is clear, there's no wind and the hot air that enters through the nose, passes through the larynx and trachea before burning the lungs. The passengers of a bus run to occupy their seats to avoid being abandoned. A 4x4 with Kuwaiti plates stops nearby. The driver, dressed in a white galabiya, red and white turban and dark police sunglasses, descends to stretch his legs while his companion murmurs tender words to a blindfolded falcon.

This is the only strip of asphalt which crosses the desolation towards Palmyra, a set of archaeological ruins so vast that admission is free. To surround and forbid entry to this local souvenir of 300 years of opulence under the Roman Empire would be useless. The ancient city, a reminder of the Silk Route with its temples, fallen columns, walls and scattered remnants of surviving buildings, occupies too many square kilometres.

Through the avenue of 1,500 Corinthian columns there once used to flow spices from India, silks from the orient, incense from Arabia, ebony, salted meat, elaborate jewellery, glassware, elephant tusks, cloudy wine and chained slaves captured in the latest war or the latest raid from the edge of the empire. All the caravans covering the road to Baghdad and the Persian Gulf, and most of those that continued to China, stopped here. Merchants became wealthy and sponsored the construction of theatres, public buildings and colonnades atop which they would set their own busts, like the great corporations of today and their sports teams.

To the north, on a hill, stands an abandoned Arab fortress. On the valley that opens out to the west is the cemetery of the nobles, a village of multi-storeyed funeral towers, Palmyra's City of the Dead. To the East, there's nothing but the immensity of the desert.

As we walk among the carved stone remnants of the *cardus maximus,* a young boy approaches and offers to sell us a camel.

"Good camel, nice camel, buy this camel!"

"I don't have money, but I'll trade the camel for her," I quickly reply, pointing to Anna.

"No!" says the boy who can't be more than twelve years old. "For her I would give you a hundred camels!"

The kid might have dirty teeth, but he's a champion. I await his laughter, at least a smile suggesting that we're just kidding around, but no, he is serious. I admit, he leaves me a bit taken aback.

"Your reply? I'm a business man!" insists the flea from below.

That night we meet him again driving a cart pulled by a horse. The next day he travels at high speed on a bicycle in front of the only standing temple, the Temple of Baal. As soon as he recognises us he slams on his brakes and he approaches casually. His large eyes open even more towards Anna.

"How are you?"

"Okay, how about you?"

"I will give you a million Syrian pounds for her!"

A million Syrian pounds would be 20,000 Euros, enough to get to South Africa with the van. I look at Anna, then the boy, I never considered it, but... I recall that several weeks have passed without any insults. The boy insists.

"Yes! A million Syrian pounds! Let's go see my brother!"

Up to this point Anna has been treated like an equal, but the desert is a big place.

"And what do you think, Anna? Can you imagine living in a tent the rest of your life? We have to know what she think of this," I suggest to the boy, who sticks out his chest.

Anna looks at him from head to toe and her smile causes the kid to stretch and grow a few centimetres in stature, he is becoming an adult before our very eyes.

"Mmmmmm... maybe, but no. Not right now," she replies. "You're still too young. But who knows, perhaps I'll return in a few years and I will marry you, not your brother."

The kid deflates with a soft snort and quickly rides away on his bicycle. There is other business to attend to. He speeds away on the Roman road, dodging crumbling columns; he turns at the reconstructed amphitheatre, and disappears.

★

During those nights, we slept in the van by the tiny garden of the Red Crescent's small dispensary. The nurses are dressed in white and are used to dealing with the human body, but they still keep their distance and smile shyly. In the afternoon there is only one man on duty.

"I'm learning English" he says lifting papers filled with very complex phrases, like 'the dromedary's stomp crushed his pneumothorax with exsanguination resulting in immediate and fatal cardiovascular arrest'.

Though he pretends to understand, he applies the old strategy of nodding even when he doesn't understand a thing. He has Indian features, or Pakistani, sallow skin, black eyes, but he's a proud Syrian and every minute that passes increases his interest in Spain.

"And you, do you have any sisters?" he asks Anna.

"Yes, one."

"How much does a woman cost in Spain?" Again.

Before giving him an answer, two shots ring out. Seconds later another shot is heard followed by the rumbling of a motor starting. I stand up, an armed man accelerates on a motorcycle towards the wall guarding the spring which dried up in 1994. Beyond that, the palm and date trees wait in a row like a firing squad.

The man stops five metres from a large white dog and without getting off his motorcycle, BAAAM! he fires. It's an execution. The dog falls backwards but continues yelping and writhing in pain. Now the executioner points at his head and fires again, BAAAM! Then he dismounts off the bike and walks towards the animal. He gives the dog a kick to make sure he's dead, and the body responds with a spasm. He is an official of death.

"They will take him away in a few hours," says the guard as we approach. "These dogs have no owners, they are dangerous, and sometimes they attack people."

At his side congregate a group of children who watch with fascination, in silence, while a female dog tortures the still warm body with bites.

"This morning he ate her puppies. He was a bad dog."

Then I remember the enraged pack of hounds that chased us for over a kilometre when we passed a nomadic camp in the middle of nowhere. They were fierce canines showing their fangs in the desert. They are a strange counterpoint to the natural hospitality of the Bedouins.

Damascus is the oldest continuously inhabited city in the world. The Umayyad mosque was once a Christian cathedral that held the sacred skull of St. John the Baptist. Before that it was a Roman temple blessed by Jupiter. Before that it was a shrine to worship the Aramaic god Hadad. Before that no one knows, but the evidence suggests it was one of the first places where man, tired of running after food, became sedentary.

What came next is what awakens you before dawn. Business owners arrive at their shops at five in the morning to mercilessly raise their metal shutters. At 5:25 the sun rises and the first call to prayer is heard, multiplied exponentially by the number of mosques in the old town. At six, the last of the businesses open and they start to rinse and sweep the sidewalks with brooms. At ten past six greetings cross the street, dozens of *salaam alaikum* find their matching *alaikum salaam* dragged through the air. Many of them filter through the fissures of ill-fitting windows and penetrate the foam pillow. At 6:40 A.M. the first traffic jams start, some drivers become impatient and lean on their horns. At seven we are likely the only residents of Damascus who are trying to sleep.

On the other side of the glass, street sellers raise their voices to get attention. The dried fruit and nut stores invade the sidewalks where women walk with their faces clear or cloudy. The butcher shops nearby display skinned goat heads next to the gold necklaces of a jewellery. At each shop there is a free-of-charge academic demonstration on the subject of haggling, with arguments for or against any given price. If you accept the first offer, typically high, the merchant has the right to feel insulted. You have taken away the craft in his job.

Before noon the call to prayer is heard again. Some men look at the time and change direction to go to the temple. A shopkeeper unfurls a small rug in front of his refreshment stand, removes his shoes and be- gins the ritual of kneeling, sitting on his heels, standing with his hands-on his knees, bowing his head, kneeling and bowing again to reach the ground with his forehead.

Portraits in a photo studio in Damascus.

The International Championship of Honking which started in Aleppo continues in Damascus. Here too there is a good chance of winning a huge trophy. I approach an optimistic policeman, who either naïvely, or as punishment, is trying to control the traffic. We look for a bus that will take us to the old quarter of Salihie, an agglomeration of madrassas, mosques and Ottoman tombs.

"I am Kurdish," he affirms before answering, noticing the magic colours of my bracelet.

A timid smile appears on his face while he dispatches a taxi that screeches to a stop to take us to Hades, or worse, to Bagdad if it were necessary.

"Otobus" he says, while looking assertively around the twelve corners of the square. *"No taxi, otobus. Otobus no money."*

Without hesitation, ignoring the traffic which threatens the rest of his remaining years, he boldly walks into the middle of the street. He is a policeman, and thus untouchable. I follow him and the drivers avoid us without casting any insults, it's marvellous. Two cars pass on the left, another on the right. Here comes a bus, it has a thin scratch next to the door. This man has marked a straight line that crosses the roundabout with traffic going in the opposite direction without even considering the possibility of an accident, the usual impatience of Syrian drivers behind the wheel, or the distraction caused by a Western woman with wavy hair. In the middle of the traffic flow he blows his whistle to stop a bus that appears at the corner. We get on and ask the price to Salihie. The driver smiles, raises his head to indicate 'No', mocks foolishly moving his hand, and signals for us to sit down in the front seats. We're foreigners, we are entitled to the front row seats, and we are welcomed.

Like an involuntary suggestion to be home, at five o'clock it's already dark. Businesses don't close but everyone is getting ready to go home. Buses speed up and get crowded, brimming with moodiness, apathy, hope, fatigue. They're as heavily laden as the sidewalks. It's been a long day. Everyone is hurrying to get to the mosque, to reunite with friends and family, to have a smoke, to shout anti-Israeli slogans, to drink another cup of sweet tea. The movement of the masses, the fluttering motion of fabrics causes a powerful stream of energy that transcends the individual and merges into a single word: urgency. Contagious urgency, even if no one is waiting you must hurry, dissolve into the rhythm, and find something. Faces dissolve, only the evening newspaper vendors remain, shouting out their chorus from the corners. Basically every city in the world is the same, you just have to change the backdrop and the costumes.

On the appointed hour a memory-old tradition is repeated, a custom that was about to disappear because of radio and television. After centuries of earthquakes, wars and revolutions, the old walls of the Al-Nofara coffee shop have settled. It wasn't easy, the planet's core moves separately from its crust, human beings are unpredictable, and it's logical that walls do not fit perfectly and finally join at such difficult angles.

The patches of yellow acrylic paint, a surface dressing applied by a sloppy nurse, covers the scars of time without hiding them. From each wall hangs a portrait, the memory of some heroic horseman, the omnipresent president, saints with stern looks and fundamental texts of the Koran painted by an artist. Sweet narghile smoke curls up to the ceiling forming thick storm clouds. The bar doesn't need decoration; it's quite enough that it continues to exist.

At every dark wooden table are two, three or four men and the same number of lukewarm glasses of tea. They discuss, some repeat energetic and confident gestures, the same you might use if you have found a way of saving the world and needed to explain it. The fortitude is audible and felt, as if it were a magnetic injection that goes into you and inoculates you with hope. Something big could happen here, you can feel it.

Suddenly a man dressed with all of Aladdin's robes walks through the door. He's wearing a Turkish fez on his head and carries a stick in his clenched fist. He settles on to a high red velvet chair and begins watching the surroundings with an exaggerated look of rage. He stares at each of us, one by one, you, him, me, us, until the bar is silent. Then he begins speaking in Arabic. I don't understand a word of it, but his hands and eyes open too far while his scimitar cuts through the air to hit a table and behead an invisible enemy. The *ooooohs!* and *aaaaahs!* of the audience are genuine and fill the air with thick laughter. He is a storyteller.

Sitting beside us is Ahmed. He owns one of the local Internet cafés that are barely tolerated by the government in Damascus and offers to guide us through the passages of the city. He wants to have that old feeling of being somewhere else, speaking another language and forget the walls are confidants of the state's Information Service. He hates being thought of as an Arab, would much prefer to be thought of as a Hittite or Aramaean, and won't shut up. He's a manifesto printed in gunpowder and resentment.

He's lived seventeen years between Europe and the United States, where he married an American. He decided to return to Syria when his father became ill, but she was refused a visa. He was told that to marry a foreigner he should have sought permission from the state beforehand. He wants to go see her, she's his wife, but he's not allowed to leave the country.

"Permission, permission, permission. After three years of separation we're now going through a divorce," he says angrily.

While we wander through the streets he continues fearlessly venting. All sorts of demons escape from his mouth. He only calms down after we go through a small door beneath an ancient carved Star of David.

A Star of David in Damascus.

We walk past fifteen metres of dark hallway and we enter into a world that suddenly seems familiar. Customers are playing cards in a central courtyard with a fountain surrounded by tiles and balconies. However, there are no guitars, no clapping hands following the rhythm of the music or sherry. Just narghile, tea, and plates overflowing with sheep testicles and brains.

A Star of David above the door of a classic Andalusian courtyard in Damascus. Sometimes history is hilarious.

"The Arabs who had the greatest influence on Al-Andalus were Umayyad. They came from Damascus," explains Ahmed on noting my surprise. "It's possible that your grandfather's, grandfather's, grandfather and perhaps a bit further on, were Arabs. Who knows, it's possible that you too carry the blood of this land, Syrian blood."

★

Some 200 kilometres to the east of Damascus is Djebel Sis, another abandoned fortress in the middle of another desert, this time a lava desert. The black rocks cover the landscape with a sinister cloak, as if death had not had enough with abandoning its skeleton in one of the most hostile environments on the planet. All around only pointed rocks remain, the cone of an extinct volcano, seven ancient tombs with walls of uneven cobblestones, and a group of exiled workers, condemned to dig a water well in the desert with picks and shovels.

It's extremely hot, so hot that we could be at the gate of the gardens of hell. Worse still, we're leaving tracks in the sand, we're walking on Satan's lawn. The prairie of Beelzebub, Belial, Leviathan, Ahriman, Iblis, Asura, Pani, Oni, Kelpies, The Boss, or whatever you want to call him. Nobody has seen him in person, but they all have a name for him. The Damned, The Angel of Darkness, The Fallen Angel, Your Worst Nightmare, Antichrist. These sharp stones are his favourite flowers. The hot dry air is his paradise. The only thing missing is a banner reading 'Welcome to the Devil's Lodge'.

I'm not sure what his calling card would look like, but it's likely to be in his local representative's language, be it English, Arabic, Russian, Chinese, Spanish or Attila the Hun's Mongolian.

When darkness falls I look for branches to start a fire. The desert is sparse, it's cruel, but it respects the courage of seeds ready to suffer in order to flourish. There will always be a new opportunity to kill something.

In Djebel Sis there has never been a forest, only brave isolated shrubs. Scorched scrubs. A few dry branches are enough to feed a small fire beneath the arch of an ancient ruined gate. A bouquet of sparks hovers over the flames and disappears a few metres away. The red hot coals shine intensely, they feel right at home. The wood creaks, writhes in pain, screaming as if I were opening a door closed with twenty bolts. At any minute the red dancer will appear.

I remember what a couple of Belgian travellers told us this morning. The 100 dollar Diesel Tax in Syria which we didn't pay when we entered the country was for each week. The official with painful constipation didn't tell us this, and we've already been here four weeks, and that's a lot of money.

I sink into the starry night and my mind jumps from the Cassiopeia Constellation to the remains of St. John the Baptist spread in museums and cathedrals all over the world. The guy did not deserve to end up like that.

Jordan is 200 kilometres by a tortuous path and 450 by a paved road that leads to the east, the north, the west, and finally south. In between is a wilderness of sharp volcanic basaltic rocks: the grasslands of Satan. The workers who are building a water well advise us to take the long route. The Bedouins who arrive at a camel's pace in a caravan of four trucks advise us to take the shorter path.

"Harram al Awamid is there, three hours, *shuei, shuei!*"

Why not risk it? Why should tomorrow be a bad day? I believe that we'll end paying the revolutionary tax though... we should cross the border at night. Furthermore, we should not go through the main border crossing, we should go by the secondary route.

"Pablo, it's not enough to know that it's in that direction. We're not going to destroy the van now just to take a shorter path. We'll have plenty of time to do that later," assures Anna, while reading the auspices in the sputtering flames of disasters crouching in Africa.

"But, don't you want to go down roads that no one ever travels?"

"Yes, of course I like to, but we need to arrive at the border quickly. Tomorrow marks the end of our fourth week in Syria. The day after tomorrow starts our fifth week. On this path we don't know the way, and it's full of sharp stones. On the asphalt there are more kilometres, but we'll get there sooner.

Only a lost cloud disturbs the clarity of the night. Lying on the irregular ground, I go over the new routines of the trip, cooking over a wood fire, writing on paper, showering every two or three days, orienting ourselves by the sun, finding the North Star before going to sleep. I have the feeling that we have too much baggage, we need to forget old habits and question situations we used to take as unquestionable truths.

We have been on the road for four months, but there are moments when time measured in hours and days ceases to have any meaning. The stars are multiplying and even the most fleeting appear like the end of a rope thrown by red and white angels from the other side.

"Did you see that shooting star?" asks Anna.

"Guess what my wish is."

"If I tell you it won't come true..."

"I asked the same thing."

When we parked at the entrance to the customs building on the Dar'a border it's been half an hour since nightfall. I'm wearing an old shirt, a full-grown beard, high morale and long hair. Anna covers her shoulders and tidies her hair. We have the script worked out, rehearsed, reviewed, and rewritten. We smile. We're an adorable couple. We have the word "innocent" tattooed on our faces. I inhale deeply and let my body relax a bit.

The first thing the Custom's Officer does after seeing our Carnet de Passage is to find his boss. The chief, somewhat obese, with a moustache, easy laughter and steaming tea in his hand does the math.

"You arrived on the fifth of October, today is November first... more or less four weeks, right?"

"Yes of course, four weeks."

"So you have to pay 400 dollars."

"What?"

"Yes, 400 dollars. The car is diesel, yes?"

"Yes."

"Taking a diesel vehicle into Syria costs 100 dollars per week. It's easy, you've been here four weeks, that's 400 dollars."

"It's not possible... when we entered the country we were told that we had to pay 100 dollars to bring the van in. They did not tell us it was by the week."

"It's the law, you have to pay up."

"But... it's not right... it's not fair. If we had known we would not have spent a week in Damascus, nor would we have accepted so much hospitality. Everyone always insisted that we should spend another night. That we could always continue tomorrow. Always tomorrow. And when tomorrow arrives, they say tomorrow again! The Syrians are too hospitable!"

These were the same sentiments which surfaced two days ago when we discovered that the tax was weekly. It's *théâtre vérité*. We've already assumed we're going to lose, but we have time, and time is the wealth of travellers. We're going to talk and stay awhile, to rummage around in his feelings of injustice and understanding until we come up with an agreement. Then we shall see what happens. The problem is that my performance was so outstanding that it has attracted too many people, military officials, civilians and tea waiters; there are too many curious spectators.

"No way! Four hundred dollars is what I earn in two months of work," embellishes Anna. "It's a lot of money. Do you think we would be staging such a spectacle if it were not so?" That part is true.

"Do you think that because we're foreigners we're rich?" I interrupt. "Well, we're not. We sleep in our van. It's our house. We don't eat in restaurants. We cook, or we eat falafel. Tourists with money pay whatever is asked of them, pay up and shut up. But we're not rich. Four hundred dollars is a lot of money!"

"You have two alternatives," says the military official. "Pay up, or return to Damascus and speak to the Big Boss."

We could phone Nouraddin and get the phone number of the lascivious colonel that was going to be promoted to Super Boss. But it might make the situation worse.

"If we have to return to Damascus, we'll return to Damascus," says Anna with conviction. "But it's completely unfair. If we pay 400 dollars, every litre of diesel purchased in Syria will have cost us more than a dollar!"

I pull out the diary where I jot down the oil changes, the number of kilometres covered each day, the names of the places where we've slept, and the litres of diesel we've purchased. We've bought 439 litres of diesel during our four-week stay in Syria.

"You think it's fair to pay a dollar a litre?"

Some of the spectators start to laugh. Then another man enters with the papers for his car.

"Is there a problem? Because we already have one here," asks the official.

"It looks like it's our problem, not yours," affirms Anna.

The official nods silently.

"It's a shame, we'll have to write about this," I say. It's time to play poker again, I look for the card up my sleeve. "We're journalists, we write about travel places and tourism. We had a nice story about Syria but now it won't have a happy ending."

Silence. For several seconds nothing moves. Then, another officer who had remained silent offers us tea, calling a boy through a window and ordering. Then he calls for some correction fluid. One of the military men gives him a dirty look. Others have suddenly left and those that stay would apparently rather be closer to the door. But no, they don't have correction fluid here. I go into the van but I can't find any. They stole it in Athens, those damn Greeks.

When I return I find Anna writing on a paper.

"They found some correction fluid."

"Really? What did they do?"

"They covered the date we entered the country and wrote another."

"That's it? Nothing else?"

"They asked for our address in Spain to visit us some day. I gave them our real direction. According to Customs, we've only been in Syria five days."

"You won't have to pay 400 dollars," says the official, "only 100, alright?"

"Certainly. It's what we have always thought. Thank you, thank you very much," I say as I shake hands, hug and kiss him on each cheek. "We'll await you in Barcelona," another embrace, "to be our guest," I say with my hand over my heart.

"Won't he be expecting some money?" asks Anna in Spanish.

He hasn't actually asked for any. If we offer him a bribe, then his gesture will not be seen as a favour done in good faith. I would rather invite him to a good paella someday.

The man stamps our travel permit with a seal.

"The exit is that way. Goodbye and *bon voyage!* Don't forget to write nice things about the people of Syria."

On the road everything is possible, I believe while I walk away trembling with joy, nerves, disbelief. We've managed to get through. God and The Devil argue over who should take credit for this miracle. The people of Syria are incredible. We start up our home and approach the immigration building dreaming of sleeping on Jordanian soil.

"We'll just cross the border and stop anywhere. With all this tension I'm trashed," I say to Anna.

Then, as we hand over our passports through a window, God and The Devil go to the bathroom. You know, incontinence affects the aged. At that moment there comes a shift. These new people, wearing an enormous smile, ask that we go with them inside. In one office there is the boss, and he's happy too, because his shift is over.

"Are you journalists?" he asks without anaesthesia.

"Well... Maybe... No... Sometimes..." Something's not right.

"On your visa renewal card from Deir ez Zor it says you're a journalist. All journalists, wherever they come from, need a special government permit to leave the country. Do you have any other paperwork?"

"No... But... I'm not really a journalist. I'm travelling and I like to write."

The night shift seems to have something to entertain themselves with. Us!

He calls up Damascus. They confirm that we have to make a compulsory visit to the director of the official newspaper, Al Jabbah, who will stamp our permit. Anna opens a door and looks in the van. Where did God go? What about the Devil? Discussions, questions and even the translation help of an Iraqi driver who is travelling to Lebanon and is being held up at the border are of no use.

"He says you are to go back to Damascus because you are a journalist."

"No, I just write, they must have misunderstood me in Deir ez Zor." "They say that you can only leave Syria with a written permit from Damascus."

"That's a stupid law," I say wearily.

"Please, don't say that. It's not wise to talk like that here."

"I'm sorry, but it doesn't make sense. It's already dark and there will not be anyone around to stamp our permit. We can't go back with our vehicle because we'll have to pay 100 dollars again, and we have already passed customs."

"They say that it's best that you go now, they are waiting for you. You should come back again tonight. It's the only solution."

We leave the van at the border and take a long-distance taxi, one of those huge American trans-Atlantic freighters from the 50s, a dull faded red affair, with a white roof and an open exhaust. An hour and a half later he abandons us in the centre of Damascus.

Damascus, again.

Anna negotiates with a Palestinian taxi-driver to get us to the newspaper office, to wait, and bring us to the centre again.

The building is an old grey tower with staircases suggesting ministerial ambitions. It rises alone, surrounded only by highways and a pretence of forest. At the reception, with dark and unreachable ceilings, there's only a man who looks at a television screen. He also greets the ghosts that come through the door.

"Ajwalan sahalan!" Welcome, he says.

"Yeah, *shukran,* thanks."

He already knows who we are. He knows why we're here. He knows who is waiting for us. All doormen know too much.

Within ten minutes some footsteps are heard. I don't know where they're coming from, the echo of huge spaces converts the footfalls of a pair of shoes into a battalion. I turn around, looking down the passages that penetrate the bowels of this bureaucracy. Nothing, just an echo. If this really were a newspaper there should be light, noise, people running around, phones ringing, the bustle of the street at dusk, the madness of tomorrow's press deadlines. But nothing, there's nothing happening. The building is immersed in semi-darkness, it's dead.

Amidst all the silence, the footsteps continue approaching. They must drag a couple of light bodies, chameleons capable of going unnoticed when necessary, men who become swirls of smoke. Empty shoes walking, without calluses, flat feet without a hint of camembert scent. Then two shadows appear on the green, imitation marble-veined tiled floors. One is tall and thin and the other is small and stooped. They are too gushing in their greeting.

"I'm sorry to disappoint you, but I'm not a journalist. There must be a misunderstanding, some confusion. I do not do interviews. I'm travelling and I like to write. That's all," I declare quickly. I want to get out of here fast.

"Ah, what a pity! Every time a reporter arrives we arrange interviews with the minister of their choice to talk about the future of Syria," says the little man.

"If you were a reporter, you'd be able to ask anything you liked with absolute freedom," adds the taller man.

"Yes, that is a tremendous shame... But I'm only a traveller. I write for pleasure, I'm heading to South Africa."

They stamp the damn piece of cellulose-yellow toilet-bond paper, as old as the regime, and we decide not to return to the border. We go back to the Zafaran Hotel, where they give us the same noisy corner room as last time.

Room number 14, just bordering on bad luck.

FIND ALL THE PHOTOGRAPHS FOR THIS CHAPTER AT
WWW.VIAJEROS4X4X4.COM

THE ENGINE OF THE EARTH

After the surreal moments of inspiration associated with the entry and exit into Syria, Jordanian customs is so proper, formal and correct that it becomes unbearably boring. Just as we finish the usual paperwork, immigration-customs-insurance, and are preparing to cross a new hurdle into another *terra incognita,* a cowboy arrives.

Butch is an Australian with blond matted locks of hair, several weeks of untrimmed beard, an old tattered hat stolen from Indiana Jones, shredded trousers and a Russian Zenit sidecar motorcycle. He moves among the border police with a confidence which no one gave him and, amid the noise of bureaucracy, his mouth twists into an evil smile. He watches, he listens, he tilts his head, smiles and shrugs with resignation: it's their rules and we're in their house.

His backstory is the same one as those of us who at some point go astray: at the age of 38 he stopped competing in the rat race. He closed the door of his old cage with five more or less assembled motorcycles

Photo: Joyous Fridays in the Jordanian desert.

and bought a ticket to Vladivostok. It was a one-way trip: he didn't want to have any commitments to anyone, not even an airline.

The last few years, since moving to the Australian Outback, had been good and quiet. Gentle. Provincials. Boring. It was what he wanted to escape the hustle and tantrums of Sydney. But then he realised that, used to the rhythm of the city, life in this idyllic village was exactly what he imagined death would be like.

With the start of the Siberian summer, he took the route to the west. He had spent several weeks going over his fourth-hand motorcycle, a cheap wreck that needed work. It was a happy moment; the intersection between the start of a journey and the end of a terrible winter in the north-eastern steppes of Asia which awakened feelings that had long been hibernating.

"Don't think the change of seasons is very noticeable; it only stops snowing for a couple of months. The frozen topsoil, the permafrost, thaws just enough to turn into mud."

He pulls out a tattered Russian atlas from 1997 that he keeps under his seat and points to a blank area which is some 1,000 kilometres to the east of Lake Baikal. It's not snow, the North Pole, or a printing error.

"The road finishes at the Amur River, which is about a kilometre wide, plus or minus a hundred metres," he says pointing forward. "There was a bridge under construction but it appeared abandoned. I travelled many kilometres on each side looking for a pontoon, a boat, or a raft of rotten logs to cross, but there was nothing. There was no one! This was as desolate as the Australian Outback. I had no choice but to backtrack and load the bike on to the train. It's the only train, the Trans-Siberian.

The autumn, much worse than our coldest winters, trapped him in Novosibirsk, to the west of Siberia. He assures us the motorcycle is his only woman, although he remembers a 20-year-old girl who wounded him badly. *She could have been my daughter, but no; there she was, at my side, in my bed.*

He travels light; he only has two shirts, a pair of trousers, a worn leather jacket, a small gas stove, and a dismantled motor in his sidecar.

He was assaulted in Vladivostok, two days after landing, where they did him the favour of stealing his watch. The only downside was waking up lying on the cold sand of the beach with a mouthful of dried blood clots. It's his first big trip and he doesn't know where he's going, he only thinks one or two weeks ahead. We saw his motorcycle in Damascus, we greeted one another in the Roman amphitheatre at Bosra, and today we set off towards a delicate spot, the Golan Heights.

★

The village of Himme is within shooting distance of the Israeli watch towers on the other side of the Yarmuk River. It's the perfect place for a nervous soldier to suffer a sudden attack of Parkinson's or fear, and start pulling the trigger. They're all within range: the children playing soccer who insult him in Hebrew, POW! The women who are shopping and despise him, POW! The men who are leaving a mosque and spit on the floor looking at him, POW! Any of them could be a suicide bomber willing to kill and die. He's been taught this, he believes it. But what causes him nightmares is to see their watchful eyes, to see the colour of the eyes of the faceless enemy right there, through his telescopic sight. Yet again, his finger begins to tremble.

The pure clean waters of the Yarmuk River, good for drinking, are poisoned. On the fence topped with barbed wires attached to the other side are warning signs in English and Arabic announcing that soldiers have orders to shoot at anyone who sets foot in the river. Beyond that there is nothing. The Golan Heights, taken from Syria by Israel during the Six Day War in 1967 is empty land – grey, barren, decrepit. On the hills grow only corroded iron towers and sharp grass which refuses to flourish until conditions change. The land is dried out by hatred.

Every half-hour a military vehicle patrols the impeccable roads built for war. Butch picks up a stone and watches the slow progress of a green jeep on the other side of the border.

"What do you bet I'll throw further than you?"

It's Friday and our arrival coincides with a flurry of words filled with anxious rage – sonic stones hurled by the loudspeakers of a mosque. I only understand *Palestine, Palestine, Palestine*. Had it not been for the impotence that persists after 40 years of continuous defeat, Himme would be just another peaceful and forgotten town engaged in subsistence agriculture.

We go into a bakery to buy some hobs, a small pita bread. Jordan was the only country that offered asylum and a new nationality to the Palestinians who lost their homes in 1967. The rest of the Arab countries refused to promote an exodus that would leave Jerusalem in the hands of the Israelis. Today, 60 percent of the population of Jordan are Palestinians, including two bakers who ask our opinion on Saddam Hussein – he of the whiskers.

"Hmmmm... he wasn't good. He started several wars and killed many people," I say.

"Nooooo. Saddam Hussein was good, very good!" they say excitedly. "He launched missiles at Israel!"

We're below sea level and Himme is not just a hotbed of revenge. The houses and shops which pop up on both sides of the asphalt do not take up much space from the orchards that produce three crops a year. Streams of warm water emerge from every crack to wet the fields surrounded by olive trees, figs and palm trees. Almost all flow into a ditch parallel to the Jordan River, so not even a drop reaches the lands cultivated by Israeli settlers.

A half mile from the village, the canal runs along a meadow separated from the asphalt by a thick row of trees. One of the problems of living on the road is showering: if you don't sweat too much you can survive some days without attracting too much attention. While we prepare to dive in, two soldiers interested in the hygiene habits of the West, appear between the trees.

They're used to women covered from head to toe, so a chance encounter with a Western woman about to take a bath in an irrigation canal is like the story-line of a porn flick that will fry their brains. Showing skin is forbidden, and a bikini is something they've only ever seen on TV. A bikini is wet underwear.

They are restless, happy. They're convinced they're invisible.

They light cigarettes and reset their stares on Anna, who remains dressed next to the van.

"Uuuuuhhh! Friday, day off... There's nothing to do!" says Butch as he gets into the water wearing his floral shorts. He opens his eyes and moves his arms like a circus announcer.

The soldiers smile.

"The water is good, hot, very hot..." Butch splashes, roiling the water. "But if you stay here, she will not enter the water. You here, she no water... understand?"

Either they don't understand, or they don't want to understand, the fact is the soldiers smile and continue smoking. The red tips glow an intense red, adolescent red after a long drag, and within seconds it turns into limp grey ash. The excitement is obvious; they're armed youths spying through the window into the girls' shower. They're excited by the appearance of a freckled shoulder. Then, Butch starts raising and lowering his fist at the height of his chest. At first it looks like a military parade, a majorette with a beard.

"I know that if she gets in the water, you'll both masturbate," he affirms while pointing with his left hand while increasing the speed of his right fist up and down, up and down. "Understand? She go water, you and you chop-chop-chop-chop!"

"No, we wouldn't do that here," reply one of the soldiers.

Butch continues raising and lowering his right arm, each time faster and with greater strength and rigidity, like a mad military automaton. His hand drops a bit more and he begins throwing water in every direction. Butch has gone crazy.

"She is not going to bathe if you stay. Go away, please," I ask laughingly. The younger soldier's face begins to change.

Their previous laxity becomes offended pride. Fierce pride. They bark at each other, they get up and move away swearing. Butch and I are egoists. Two minutes later an armed soldier shows up with orders to kick us out.

We finally bathe at another bend several kilometres down the road. When we have finished dressing ourselves a young man appears with a shotgun. He's late. Or he was hidden. He approaches as I finish putting on my trousers. He speaks some English, so I ask him what he's doing here with that rifle. A fraction of a second later I realise that he could answer 'I assault foreigners'.

"I'm hunting rabbits while I guard the sheep," he responds.

I breathe a sigh of relief.

"Are there many?"

"Yes, many. Enough for me not to work," he says.

He notices that I'm looking at him with curiosity.

"Work, work. Everyone works and when the end of the month comes, what's left in your pocket?"

"Depends... sometimes something, other times nothing."

"Exactly, sometimes nothing. So, why work? I take sheep on walk, carry shotgun and hunt rabbit for dinner. My wife prepare, then I visit friends. If necessary I hunt more rabbits or sell fat sheep. Simple."

In the year 500 AD most of the inhabitants of the Middle East only believed in the gods who came down to earth. Turkey, Syria, Jordan, Lebanon, Palestine, Israel and a good part of the southern Mediterranean embraced the teachings of Jesus of Galilee, the revolutionary rabbi who had proclaimed himself to be the Son of God. Cobbled Roman roads linked the provinces of the old Empire and dirt paths opened out in all directions to facilitate the expansion of trade, ideas, faith and soldiers. Traffic in the surrounding Dead Sea was intense, everyone wanted to know the country of the latest great prophet, who had died and risen again on the third day after announcing: "All men are created equal!"

This was indeed a novelty. In those days you had to have courage to speak up and say that aloud.

In one of those ancient crossroads stands Amman, a trivial farming town that in 1921 became the capital of the emirate of Transjordan. The remains of that little village, old Amman, is the noisy capital of modern Jordan.

We always park in front of Wasfi's kiosk. Wasfi is a full man in his 40s, with a round and friendly face. He sells wooden boxes from India, fake leather belts, shiny brass plates with the 99 names of Prophet Mohammed, small lighters with two flames, and mirrors with the image of Virgin Mary and Prophet Isa, which is what the Muslims call Jesus Christ. He also has a picture of the Last Supper where the only one with the holy halo is Isa. The apostles were mere mortals.

"Careful with Iraqis," he warns when we sit down at his side for the first little glass of tea for the day. "Some not good. Here, almost all shops are Palestinian. Here, in the centre, almost no Jordanians. Only Palestinians and tourists. King Hussein, too good."

Fifty yards away stand the ruins of a small Roman amphitheatre. People cross the street with bottles of Coke in their hands, it's hot. Birds open their beaks to chirp, but no one can hear them.

A serious-faced man with a large beard and black galabiya approaches, followed by four women who are so covered up you could well doubt their gender. They are probably his wives, the four which he's allowed by law.

With the excuse that we're travelling around the world, the Ministry of Tourism gives us both free passes to enter museums and Jordan's Protected Areas. A stranger from Saudi Arabia pulls out his wallet with a folding section of at least fifteen credit cards and pays for half of two new Bridgestone tires for us; *if you want to get to South Africa you'll need good ones, not the cheap kind.* The manager of a garage gives us tools we don't have. The basis of Western civilisation is effort, in Arab countries solidarity is more important.

The Koran commands the poor must be helped, slaves must be freed and everyone must commit to the will of God. It also compels followers to help those beset by debt, those who need to reconcile their hearts and yes, those who travel. The Koran was written some 1,400 years ago when the only reason for travelling was commerce or faith. To move from one region to the next could be the adventure of a lifetime.

Unlike Europe, where people just give what they have left, in Arab countries people give what they have. You don't see the homeless begging in the street, no one cries on their knees for a piece of bread or a bowl of lentils. There is no need to humiliate yourself.

In Islam, God, Allah, is present in a person's every act. Every sentence that expresses a future action always ends with *inshallah,* if it is the will of Allah. Every action is always ended with *al-hamdulillah,* thanks to Allah, even if the result was a disaster. No good Muslim will tell you he's going to do something in the next ten minutes, three hours or seven days without finishing the sentence with inshallah. It would be blasphemy.

Thus, when the finance minister said the pockets of citizens will be better within a year, it is always conditional on the will of God. *Inshallah.* When an employee announces that he will make a photocopy, it will also be *inshallah.* When he returns with the copies, it will be *al-hamdulillah,* thanks to Allah.

The best example is the radio. Listeners who call in spend half the conversation with inshallahs and al-hamdulillahs, the only words I understand. All the successes and failures, advances and setbacks, will be the result of the will of God, not man's will.

Life is written in an invisible book called destiny. Nothing can change the future.

★

Our life in Amman revolves around Zahran Avenue, the asphalt line connecting the centre with the diplomatic quarter. Every time we look for an alternate way to avoid another traffic jam, we get lost. We go in circles around the hills of the city, we take turns through narrow passages with directions in Arabic and we finish in dead end lanes at the top of the hills. There is nothing for it, to move through Amman you must follow your destiny, the path is marked. Here too you must apply the law of patience, one of the unwritten rules of coexistence in Arab countries.

When it gets dark we go back to sleep in the embassy area. It's a new neighbourhood of quiet streets, low buildings of grey and white blocks, modern brick houses and small commercial centres with North

American ambitions. Amman has prospered considerably by virtue of its alignment with US foreign policy.

The third night we wake up after some firm knocks on the windows. It's 5 a.m. and two policemen think the van looks suspicious.

"Good morning," says the policeman.

"Good morning? It's still dark out!" I answer in a bad mood.

"What are you doing here?"

"I'm sleeping. What do you think people do at this hour?"

After five minutes of a curious tug of war, they leave. Half an hour later the sky begins to lighten, the sun is still hidden, but the light filters through the windows and our eyelids become translucent. As much as I want to keep my eyes closed, I can no longer sleep. I know I'm not dreaming, but I'm not awake. Tired and dazed, I only manage to put on a coat before sitting on the sidewalk and leaning against the wall of a vacant lot, another great green patch in a cage. Fifteen years ago, flocks of sheep grazed here.

I open the book 'Sands of Arabia' by Wilfred Thesiger, but my head can't join words, it's too early.

Anna is still asleep.

On the other side of the street there's a group of nice homes. The closest has a green garden filled with flowers and a shiny, late model BMW. On this side there is a low building with large balconies enclosed with glass. The curtains are drawn open on one of them, revealing sofas and framed Miró posters over walls painted in pastel colours. It's not too different from what we would find back home.

It's cold, winter has arrived and I'm beginning to sympathise with those vagabonds with dirty clothes and uncomfortable bodies after a week of only minor daily washings. I watch the building and remember hardwood floors, warm rugs, movies, decent libraries, a fridge with freezer, overstuffed sofas, a bathroom. A shower!

"You can't be like this," I repeated a year ago to the TV that was proclaiming news that wasn't mine. Having your head in one place and your body somewhere else, forgetting what's important and turning accessories into indispensable items. Day dreaming and opening your eyes to start again like a damn robot that wakes up under the automatic control of routine!

I lived in a large and comfortable apartment and had a job that was difficult to leave. The price of submission was paid for in frustration. I was being disloyal, and to add insult to injury, I was getting fat.

I'll never forget that Monday when I put the barrel of a gun to my head and fired until I was out of bullets, not stopping to think what I was doing so as not to change my mind. It was my resignation to a future I already knew, a farewell to a secure job, an adieu to a brilliant career in advertising, the microcosm where I'd lived for the last twelve long years. It was ten minutes after ten in the morning and my last words were, more or less "keep the corpse, I'm leaving." My body collapsed and I walked out the door.

When the first light comes on in a window, I imagine what those last tender cuddles must feel like in a real bed. *Is it already six?* Someone gets out of a warm bed with feather duvets and soft music playing on the radio. Someone drags themselves to the kitchen and automatically turns on the coffee maker. Someone pushes a button to make toast. Someone pulls a carton of milk from the fridge and has a drink. We are all made up of rituals and routines.

Then, with my back straight and leaning against the cold wall of a vacant lot, I understand the horror of the vagabond being forced on to the street. Incredulous, avoided, wasted, a nobody, fully aware of having been fired from an anonymous society. Harassed by the police. Shunned by people. Not entitled to any compensation or social welfare. Around me are men are in a hurry to finish a day that hasn't started, apathetic children crawling to school, women vomiting to look better, and plastic flowers on tables.

A year after my commercial suicide, routine consists of figuring out where we're going to sleep tonight, eating when the body is hungry and negotiating with Fortune about when we'll find a bathroom. Every day is different from the day before and that's almost always good. The road entwines us in its unwritten stories of humanity converted into statistics. Stories that don't appear in any travel guides.

It's sunrise in Amman.

The light from the east filters obediently through the atmosphere. The forecast is for clear skies and brutal heat. As I pass my hand over my face to dislodge my eyelids, I notice my cheeks are rough. I should find a public washroom and shave.

"Mister! Mister! Police! What are you doing here! Hotel! Go to a hotel!" I yell while I balance on the old, square, red, all-terrain vehicle belonging to Jorick and Winnie, the Belgians we met in Syria.

We found them sleeping in one of the seven hills of Mount Nebo, the natural viewpoint where Moses discovered the Promised Land. The scenery is breathtaking. A ruined house marks the north while a bunker, a reminder of the Six-Day War, marks the west. The soil is rocky and a few stunted trees keep their composure before the dizzying drop that starts some metres away and ends abruptly in the Dead Sea. On the horizon shine the lights of Jericho, the Jordan River valley and a whole tableau of fireflies, white in Jordan and yellow in the West Bank or Palestine or Israel. It's easy to see where the border is.

Jorick and Winnie are thin, very thin. It seems essential to live in their little Old Faithful, the Land Rover Series 1 with the demonic registration number GEE666. He displays his thinning hair with pride; he's an engineer and in his previous life drove large machines in a Belgian port. He likes tinkering with machinery and is incredulous that we're going to cross Africa without knowing so much as how to repair a flat. We connect fast and if we ever have any issues with our four-wheel drive, he's always willing to lend a hand.

Winnie seems like she's about to break. She studied psychology, has brown hair and is really beautiful. She's 1.7 metre and she can't weigh more than 50 kilos, which is a bit dangerous during a long trip: the slightest infection or illness can weaken you. A bite from a malaria-infected mosquito could be fatal. She must be a tough woman despite her delicate looks and her house-wife-presenting-a-birthday-cake smile.

Before seeing their faces at the entrance to the folding roof tent that's permanently mounted on the Land Rover, *"man-oh-man, what are you doing here?"* I hear a groan. It comes from the ground, inside a cardboard box. Two weeks ago they dodged a fuzzy lump and a shattered body on the asphalt of a Syrian road. When they looked back, the fuzzy lump moved.

"It's an Arab shepherd puppy... rather, it was a great tick," explains Jorick, with feet now planted on the ground. "When we picked him up, he was still looking for his mother's nipples in a mass of run-over flesh. He was starving to death. We found him in Bosra, and that's what we call him, Bosra."

The fuzzy lump became a hairy ball that travels on top of the spare wheel or on Winnie's lap. They vaccinated him against distemper, rabies, leptospirosis, hepatitis and bad luck so they could travel with him across borders. But nothing could protect him against children without a foot-ball. For Muslims, dogs are as dirty as pigs.

We park nearby, we look for wood to light a fire, and we open a bottle of Arrack which we keep under the mattress. We have to celebrate the reunion. *"What happened at the Syrian border?"*

Past midnight, hours after the embers have burnt out, the van begins to shake. I open my eyes, and look outside. It's not the revenge of Jorick, no. It's the wind, which must have begun as the gentle sway of a nanny who ended up going crazy. The wind blows with a strength that I had never before witnessed, as if it wanted to drag us down towards the Dead Sea.

I open the door. The tent where the Belgians are sleeping is still in place, as is Bosra's box. The small bent tree that is close by loses one of its branches while trying to protect itself from the violence of the wind. It's not easy walking in the dark over uneven ground while a furious wind tries to push you along. I check everything to make sure all is in order. The canvas which covers the roof luggage remains secure, and the bag with ten litres of drinking water hasn't fallen and broken into a thousand liquid pieces. Anna's grandmother's battered pot with the remains of dinner has escaped down the mountain. The lid will be further away. The loose ends move hysterically towards Israel or Palestine, as if all the fury of the world wanted to concentrate itself on a new intifada. I don't know if it's a prediction or a windy monologue which whispers an endless mantra.

"I'm Patagonian, I'm Icelandic, I'm Siberian, I am strong and hard and cold and I'm going to continue cutting short your dreams with rushes of wind at night, without haste, without pause, without mercy. I'm Patagonian, I'm Icelandic, I'm Siberian, I am strong and hard and cold..."

"Oil is not the greatest wealth of Arabs," I assure Gareb and Mona, who live with their nine children in an unfinished house in Wadi Musa, close to Petra. "If you could export hospitality, give it a shape and package it, the Arabs would be able to make more money than by selling oil."

We knocked on their door to refill the propane cylinder for our stove, thinking it was Thursday. We quickly realised that we had once again lost a day somewhere; it was Friday and everything was closed. Tuesday, Wednesday or Thursday had disappeared in a bend of the road. Gareb not only opened his business and didn't want to charge

Gareb, Mona and some of their children at Wadi Musa, close to Petra.

us forthe propane, but invited us to dinner and to stay overnight in his home, have breakfast with his family, and stay as long as necessary.

"No problem. We don't have much, but if eleven can eat, so can 13. You can sleep in this room. The van can remain on the street, nothing will happen to it. Everyone here knows me and respects me. You are my guests, so you are also Gareb. I'm sorry, but we don't have a shower. If you need hot water, we'll heat it and you can wash up in this tub. Are you hungry? Would you like some tea? A coffee?"

In this part of the world, hospitality is as natural as breathing. If you step into a shop it's logical the merchant insist on selling you something. If you don't buy anything, most will invite you to sit down for a glass of tea so you can tell them a story.

I discuss this with Gareb and Mona, who have more children than money, and they smile. I tell them that in Europe and the United States this is not very common. City people are usually suspicious. Children do not approach strangers. People close their doors rather than open them.

Gareb doesn't understand this.

"But...if I open the door of my house it's because you're on your way, because you'll have things to tell... if I invite you into my house, it's because I don't know you... I have no reason to distrust you."

★

Petra is one of the ten places of the world you should visit before dying.

We take along some water, a pot of nougat with nuts called *halawa*, a plastic bottle with three litres of yogurt, and an urge to walk. The first Westerner to reach Petra did so by lying.

Jean Louis Burckhardt, a stubborn Swiss, was near Karak in 1812 when he overheard a conversation between some Bedouins about a secret town surrounded by impenetrable mountains. He had been living and dressing like an Arab for years, but his accent gave him away as a foreigner. So, he introduced himself as a pilgrim from the north, where all the deserts ended. He was looking for a guide to help him fulfil the promise of sacrificing a goat in the sacred temple of the prophet Aaron, may Allah keep him in his glory.

It wasn't easy to get to the *Siq*, a little dry canyon a bit more than four metres wide and 60 high, an ideal spot to get ambushed. Along the way, the Liyathneh tribe and his personal guide tried to convince him to sacrifice his goat at other temples; The Prophet rewards acts, not places. However, Burckhardt insisted on entering the *Siq*.

The first surprise comes from the sandstone walls, which range in colour from a violent flame to purple sunsets to mandarin oranges as they begin to ripen. Thousands of years of wind have polished the walls to such an extreme that your fingers feel like they're caressing skin, a newborn infant's skin. The floor, carpeted in sand and gravel, glides smoothly without interruptions or sharp inclines. Only the horse-drawn carriages loaded with rosy tourists inclined to the abuse of exclamations disturb the timeless silence. Small eroded sculptures and niches appear in a corner as a hint of what's to come.

Suddenly you feel a whiplash, a concussion, a surprise which straightens your back. I open my mouth in an attempt to react, but words escape me. At the end of the crack, under a golden light, appear the first glimpses of The Treasury. On both sides of the shafts which keep the doors open to the heart of the mountain are stairs chiselled into the vertical rock. The slaves who worked here had no choice but to be acrobats.

The movie 'Indiana Jones and The Last Crusade' was the best advertising campaign for Petra. That matinee multiplied tourists dreaming of losing themselves amid the facades carved by the Nabataeans in the desert. You only have to look at the walls on each side of kilometres of desolate valleys to appreciate the magnitude of the work. The vision is so powerful that, before signing the peace treaty with Jordan, Israeli youth used to take up a dangerous challenge: cross the militarised border, arrive clandestinely at Petra, and return to Israel with a coloured stone. Sometimes they never returned; sometimes they simply vanished.

Tahal is 23 years old and works in one of the many bends of Petra's *Siqs*. His stand is laden with handicrafts and antique coins. It's not a bad business. He's a nice guy and he wants to sell us something, but finally he takes a rest and invites us for tea.

"Twenty years ago, my tribe, the Bdul, were living in the caves of Petra. I was born there. We had our camels, our goats and we lived without any worries for anything else. We didn't need any more. We were happy, as free as our ancestors," he says, and pauses a moment, recalling times which he has not lived. He takes a sip of tea and continues.

"Petra was part of our lands. But the government kicked us out and gave us square houses. My mother liked the change; the houses had running water and electricity. There was no more carrying buckets of water or lighting fires. Progress had come to our family. But, you know? I look at the past and I compare it to the present and I feel that we ended up losing. Now we no longer walk through the desert with our camels and goats, we no longer seek fresh pastures and springs. Now we just sell postcards to tourists."

His words continue in my head when we leave the asphalt and take a detour marked only by the tracks of Bedouin four-wheel drives. I don't know if this is the path we're supposed to take, but perhaps it is. It doesn't matter, *the important thing is the journey, destiny is always a surprise,* I repeat, as a cloud of dust rises in the rear-view mirror. There aren't any signposts on the sides of the old track, the only thing that shows we're going in the right direction is a compass that should be pointing east but goes crazy from all the potholes. The map is only useful to show that somewhere to the north there's a main road.

Dark spots resembling moisture transform the slopes of the hills into molten and burnt chocolate cakes. Wadi Rum is a maze of parallel valleys with overhanging balconies in unexpected places. They serve as theatre boxes for vultures who watch the passage of exotic meat. Without doubt, they wish the worst for us.

Deeper tracks lead us to the foot of a natural stone bridge some 15 metres high. We cross canyons and ravines, and pass lonely trees that shade carpets of green goat dung. A Bedouin tent woven out of some kind of brown hair appears in a bend in the road. It must be empty, nobody exits. Twice we had to look for a different valley: when we ran into a giant sand dune that had eaten the tracks and when we realised we were at risk of hearing a helicopter repeating in Arabic, English and Esperanto that we have illegally crossed into the territory of Saudi Arabia. We're very close.

At nightfall we camp behind a dune, though taking the decision is easier than getting there. It takes 40 minutes to get out of a sand trap and advance 30 metres. While Anna moistens some hard bread with a pair of tomatoes passed their prime, I rearrange the inside of the van into sleep mode and round up some wood to start a fire. Unfortunately there are no trees here either, only scrawny bushes with as many thorns as a hedgehog. Small spinal columns, broken ribs which burn in quick flashes, go out as if they never existed.

There is something exceptional in this stillness, in this unexpected death. I look around, scratch the thick evening air, nothing. Night falls silently in Wadi Rum. There is no wind, the skeletons of vegetation stand still, the sand rests on its way to the next dune. Nothing. This is also a desert of sound.

I shake one of the grey branches I carry in my hand.

The amazing desert of Wadi Rum

Sssssssss..., buzzz. *Crack,* it splits.

I find a flat rock to sit on and wait for the return of the music. At any moment the planet will finish checking over its engines and someone will turn the ignition key. Only then will the planet continuing crunching along.   ★

★

★

At dawn on the third day it starts to rain. A downpour in the desert is an event. The few leaves on the shrubs wash off their layer of dust, scorpions dilute their poison, the shells of armour-covered seeds soften, the soil moistens, there is hope. I look out through the window at the wavy sky, covered in traces of blue, grey, orange and white, Renoir, Monet, Van Gogh, who art in heaven, and I leap out naked to photograph mountains covered in gold.

When the last drops smash against the roof of the van, an anxious silence once again takes hold of Wadi Rum. Seconds later an imperceptible breeze begins to whisper through the open door, the red sand rages and the thorny bushes shudder. The purity of the light becomes religious. Then the birds return. It makes sense that Judaism, Christianity and Islam were all born near here. Even sceptics become mystics with these convulsions of nature.

Soon, the intemperate singing voices of two Bedouins approach. They announce their arrival, there are no doors here. They're riding on two beautiful white male camels, tied together with a rope to two female camels and a calf that pursues her mother's udder.

"Having problem?" asks one of them.

"No, why?"

"Being stopped here. Nobody stop here."

"The desert is beautiful."

After a minute of indecision, *I was waiting a different response,* he takes out a cigarette and lights it. I ask him if he's observing Ramadan.

No response, he just shrugs and continues smoking.

Ramadan started two mornings ago. Thirty days of fasting, hunger and thirst between sunrise and sunset, while a ball of fire slowly sounds the sky over your head until the first stars appear on the horizon. Then, new songs arrive with the wind. Another group of Bedouins approach slowly on their animals.

Anna boils water for tea. Today we have visitors at home.

★

Few chassis manage to cross the speed hump of the entry to the port of Aqaba without creating a few sparks. It's not that it's too high or too anything, the problem is one of weight; too much of it. The taxis and old trucks arrive fully loaded with passengers, blankets, televisions, suitcases, bicycles and packages bearing names written in Arabic. *In this box is Qassim's life and he's moving to Egypt.*

Everyone stops in front of a truck trailer that's being used as a baggage hold on the ship, where a corpulent brown-skinned black-moustached fellow is giving out receipts without checking the packages. *Free! Receipts are free! Come and see! Forward Sir! Afterwards we'll raffle bags, packages and bicycles! There's something for everyone!* Trucks from Kuwait, Syria, Jordan and Egypt wait like obedient hounds to cross the Red Sea with drivers crowned with different *keffiyeh* headdress. The pattern doesn't depend on what's fashionable, but rather on the tribe.

We could all use the road through the southern fringe of Israel, no more than ten kilometres between the last Jordanian and the first Egyptian outpost. However, the Israeli military inspections are exhaustive, the closest thing imaginable to being outrageously abusive: you have to empty your vehicle completely and submit to lengthy individual interrogations about your intentions.

"Why are you visiting Israel? What's in your luggage? Are you against the existence of the State of Israel? Do you carry firearms, explosives or radioactive material? What is your relationship with the woman you're travelling with? Why do you have a radio? What does this paper say?"

I have no desire to convince a stranger that I'm innocent. I have no wish to have problems getting into Sudan with an Israeli stamp on my passport.

The third option is to cross from Saudi Arabia into Yemen, and then take another boat to Djibouti. But we're in Ramadan – millions of Muslims from all over the world are gathering in Mecca in an act of ritual purification. Mecca, which is on the way, will become a fiery volcano of faith. Lava dressed in white, energy in its purest state willing to spill out into every corner of the world. Only for this reason alone they might not give us a visa. The ferry to Nuweiba, Egypt, loaded with passengers that leave their hungry bodies on deck, is a good choice.

'Ramadan is the month when the gates of heaven remain open and the devil is in chains.' You have to move less, sweat less, endure the unbearable urge to smoke, and not touch any woman. Patience. On the radio we hear female voices frightened because their husbands accidentally brushed against them and are asking if that will condemn them to hell. There is no water, what is that Christian putting into his mouth before the yellow eyes of those who sleep in the shade? No, there isn't any, "it's just a mirage" they whisper with a pasty tongue. Fortunately, this year Ramadan occurs in winter, with shorter days and bearable heat.

We set sail an hour later. Four Germans start playing cards on the deck near the bow and twenty brown faces watch over them. To look is not a sin. A man forgets fasting and peels an orange with his wife, morbidly obese and with enough make up to attend Carnival in Rio de Janeiro. We pass a ruined fortress built on a tiny island barely above the water. The wash from our boat splashes against its stone walls. Three men look at the orange peeler with anger, at any minute they're going to toss him into the sea. *Pig overboard!*

There's nothing to do but read and watch. Some sleep with their chins sunk into their chests, others talk, and still others appear to be in a catatonic state. They don't do anything. The deck is wide and spacious, but there's not a single free spot in the shade to lean up against. The interior is worse, it's like a crematorium with a low fire, there must be a direct connection to the engine room. The bar is closed because of Ramadan. Anyway, I doubt that they would have sold cold beer during the rest of the year. The sky is clear and only the murmur of the warm, transparent water breaks the monotonous silence. There is nothing to do, nothing, except watch the straight line of the Red Sea surrounded by desert. Port and starboard, Egypt and Saudi Arabia, sand and more sand.

Some young Syrians offer me sweets from an open box. I decline, but they laugh and help themselves. *Better, more for us.* After a couple of routine questions they ask for our address in Barcelona, you never know where life will take you.

"My home is my van."

"Well then, your telephone number."

"I don't have a phone," which is true, though to them that's a blatant lie. It is impossible not to have a telephone in Europe.

Time passes slowly, almost motionless.

Some hours later the sun plunges on the horizon. The speakers on the deck begin to crackle, shaking off the lethargy of a long day. Someone hits a microphone which causes a long, whistling feedback loop that awakens the ones who were slumbering. Then we hear the voice of a man reciting prayers, tackling the words with a sombre sincere melody.

Night falls, the first star appears on the horizon. Another day of fasting ends on the Red Sea.

FIND ALL THE PHOTOGRAPHS FOR THIS CHAPTER AT
WWW.VIAJEROS4X4X4.COM

THE UNFORGETTABLE ROADS OF BABEL

There is no god but God and Mohammed is his prophet... There is no god but God and Mohammed is his prophet... There is no god but God and Mohammed is his prophet...

The Islamic mantra continues its decrescendo until it's devoured by hunger. Then all the passengers on the boat pounce on the lunch bags they've brought from the mainland. The road to the stomach, opened by the first star of sunset, is clear. *Falafel, hummus, mahshi* or *sakhan* sounds better than fried mashed chickpea puree, vegetables stuffed with rice squashed together in a bag or chopped up baked chicken -- luke-warm from the sun's heat. The result is the same: much chewing and several small burps of satisfaction.

Conversations fade as the coast dissolves away. On the left, Saudi Arabia is a dark mystery. On the right, a few dwindling lights light up the night in Egypt. Above, the Universal Light Company ignites the stars again, which are fleetingly reflected on the water's surface.

Photo: Shepherds at the Camel Market in the outskirts of Cairo.

After eight hours of rocking in a crowded, uncomfortable cradle, with hundreds of men and women renewing their commitment to Allah, we arrive at the port of Nuweiba. Nu-wei-ba. The name sounds good, it has the rhythm of an exotic premonition, of some legendary African princess, even though Sinai is the Asian appendix of Egypt. We follow the line-up of four-wheeled animals that exits from the stomach of the ferry like trained circus elephants. But there is no fanfare, just a director who dryly points at us and directs us towards a dark parking lot at the end of the port. We're not alone; a casual conglomeration of Libyans, Tunisians, Belgians and Qataris waits in parked disarray.

"Egyptian customs only understands the romance of green bills," says a Tunisian to anyone who will listen while he rubs his thumb with his index finger.

"How long will we be here?" I ask.

"All the time Allah and the custom agents want. Two, three, four hours. Perhaps we'll be here forever. You know, in these places you have to pray not only to the God in Heaven," replies a discouraged voice.

A weak light comes on at the end of a dark corridor. I recognise a dust-covered Russian sidecar motorcycle under a corrugated iron roof. It's Butch's girlfriend. The Australian couldn't have crossed this border without a Carnet de Passage en Douane.

After a while, two officials poke their heads through a door and look, with a hundred-yard stare, at the used cars bought in Qatar bound for Libya and Tunisia, and the European four-wheel drives bound for Africa. Slowly, the gears of bureaucracy begin to squeak. Forms have to be filled out, signed and sealed at various windows, photocopies have to be made, returned while waiting in random line-ups, line up here, line up there, a signature, another photocopy, more money.

"Those bastards!" yells Anna four hours later, while reading the numbers written in Farsi on the visa stamped in the passport.

The three months granted by the Egyptian Embassy in Amman were capriciously reduced to merely fifteen days. We paid more than 300 euros for customs to enter the van into Egypt, 60 euros for two months of coverage with the Pharaonic Insurance Company, 12 euros for the privilege of owning a temporary yellow license plate written with red Farsi numbers, and six euros for five photocopies. Ink is extraordinarily expensive here. Jorick and Winnie, our Belgian friends, paid a special twelve euro tax at another office which no one asked us for. It's the *Having Been Born Further North Tax.*

At the port's exit gate they ask for some *baksheesh*, a tip because they were friendly and they didn't necessarily have to be. Only then do they open the last barrier. At midnight we immerse ourselves in this new unknown land to find a place to sleep.

★

At six in the morning reality is a drowsiness which resembles the second part of a dream. I think we're in Egypt. It's sunrise, that's certain.

I still hesitate, in doubt, when I open the door to see where we parked last night. Anna grumbles and turns to go back to sleep. In the rolling hills of sand, I see tiny chunks of what I assume is coral scattered amid great abandoned seashells. On the dunes there are huts measuring four square metres, behind are flesh-coloured mountains. Towards the sun, which climbs the horizon to the east, is the Red Sea. After that there's a fine line of dirt; Saudi Arabia remains in place. The cold sand runs slowly through my toes which splay open, reminding me that at one time we didn't wear shoes. Not far away, a wooden board with a hand-painted rainbow and a butterfly proclaim CENTER DUNE. CAMP + RESTO. ADAM. My neurones have just finished doing their check-up diagnostic and are now trying to do their job. I doubt that will happen before I have a coffee.

While I awaken, the blues of the sea tinge themselves in green and the greens become turquoise. There are no ships, the salt water of the Gulf of Aqaba lies on the shore without emotion, without rising or falling, and without producing those lapping waves that make children frolic. It's a warm pool, though enormous. The surf, twenty metres away, crowns the geography between the known and the unknown, the infinite plane which hovers above the water of this submerged land. Below are mountains, valleys, coral trees and flying fish.

A tall man, strong and black, comes out of a shack and approaches hesitantly. His face takes up the only space left from a Scottish scarf that covers his head. He's wearing a jean jacket that's a bit tight, perhaps one size too small. He walks slowly, dragging his feet in sandals that proclaim the triumph of plastic over leather. His whiskers are streaked with grey, as is the little hair that remains on his bald Franciscan head. His eyes emanate a gentle curiosity.

He's the Adam from the sign. Born in Sudan, he lives off 20 per cent of the revenue from the small bar that he runs, the other 80 per cent goes directly to the Bedouin owners. But now there is no revenue. Nothing. The undeclared war between the Israelis and the Palestinians keeps the Egyptian border closed to Jews, their main customers. The beaches are deserted.

"Europeans go further south to Sharm el Sheik. They like hotels, not these wood and straw huts," he says with resignation.

Adam explains how nine years ago he established himself in Nuweiba, first working in the kitchen of a restaurant, afterwards in another, and finally on his own empty patch of beach. He lived for many years in Saudi Arabia, a few years less in Libya, and if he gets enough money together, he'd like to move to Nepal, even though it's cold. Then he adjusts the scarf which covers his head as if just the name was enough to lower the temperature.

Nuweiba is a paradise. There's absolutely nothing here, not even street sellers. Only huts with palm leaf roofs, calm water, fine sand, and several Sudanese people with open and easy-going hearts. A couple of kilometres away, by way of a soft trail, is the village, the only place where I can buy *hobs,* a round flatbread. We've decided to share Ramadan and all schedules are now changed. Lunch, for example, starts as the first star becomes visible, at five o'clock in the afternoon.

Then, extremely punctually after twelve hours of fasting, Adam prepares a spread on a low table consisting of two large plates of *ful* and *asida:* sautéed green beans with onions, tomatoes, spices and lots of garlic, accompanied by a flour paste sprinkled with water that he's boiled on the fire. The cutlery is the fingers of the right hand.

"Eat, eat please, I made enough for everyone," he assures us with an honest smile when Taf Taf arrives. He's a young Sudanese who lives on the beach.

With empty plates and an empty mouth it's inevitable that everyone speaks of home, the terra firme of travellers and expatriates. We still have a lot to go through before we think of the van as more than just a vehicle. Spain is discussed and analysed before we begin taking notes on Sudan, the largest country in Africa.

"I doubt you'll be able to visit the south, there's a war going on. It's impossible to go further than Kosti."

"Why is there a war?" asks Anna.

"Because the south wants to separate from the north. Blame it on the English. In the north, people speak Arabic and the language of their tribe. In the south, people speak English and as well, the language of their tribe. In the north, we're Muslims and in the south they're Christians. But it's not a religious problem. Some countries don't have a good opinion of our government and want to divide us, encouraging southern leaders to rebel. As well, there's oil in the south."

He pauses and keeps a vacant gaze on nowhere or in Sudan, wherever it might be.

"Africa is not like Europe. People belong first to their tribe and secondly to their country. They must defend their tribe above everything else, whether it makes sense or not. If the leader of the tribe says you have to fight, you fight. If it's your turn to die, you die."

"In Sudan there are more than 700 tribes," interrupts Taf Taf. "For example, I'm a Dinka, well, not exactly, I'm from a smaller tribe in Dinka territory, and Adam is Bagghara."

"Everyone here is from a different tribe but in the end we're all Sudanese," says Adam. "In Nuweiba we are about thirty and almost all of us work on the beach. Whenever a Sudanese arrives, we come running to welcome him, no matter the hour or if he's from the north, south, east or west. He's Sudanese and will always be welcome to a plate of food and a place among us. This is true whether it's in Nuweiba, Berlin or New York.

"Certainly," affirms Taf Taf. "No matter where you are, when you know one Sudanese, you know all of them."

★

Accustomed as we are to being constantly on the move, Nuweiba is one of those places that's capable of spoiling a good overland story for one of routine breezes, grilled fish and poor firewood from the desert. Every day the darkness accommodates itself around another pot of sweet tea shared amid the light of the flames from another fire, the same as yesterday and the day before. The hypnotic murmur of the sea receding and returning slowly saps our will to continue rolling along once we landed. Should we stay or should we go? Should we stay or should we go? The rhythm of the journey intensifies but we let it pass. It's impossible to leave the beach, it's impossible to leave this beach.

"We're buried in sand, like in Wadi Rum, but this time it's harder to leave. It's not enough to dig our way out or put down the aluminium tracks," I say to Anna when we try explaining this paralysis.

The reality is much simpler: we have found a spot. One of those few places in the world where time stops and passes unnoticed.

Under the clear warm water there is an abundant inundated orchard inhabited by schools of fish that play at scaring you when they move like the shadow of a shark. In this garden you can fly over forests of soft corals in every colour which sway gently. The flooded Rift Fault descends to the centre of the earth in breathtaking blue cliffs. The underwater landscape is so spectacular that if Adam and Eve had had gills, the Garden of Eden would have been here.

Every day is the same on the yellow earth. But no matter, night eventually falls and the image of lunch after finding the first star is repeated. *There, over there, on the horizon.* You sit on the ground in front of a low table and you share the food with someone you barely know but who has opened the doors of his hut like a new brother of

Sudan. You showed up out of nowhere and the "why" doesn't matter. *Sit at my table, eat, drink.* Yet again.

I stray away from the fire and direct my conversation to the sea, towards those few monotonous notes that are constantly repeated, unchanging. One of those nocturnal dogs that bite people who don't pay the daily tribute of pats on the head approaches. He recognises me and wags his tail. Then the shaking starts. The thrill of travelling again bursts into thousands of particles that cause an intense vibration in the air. The dog of habits watches me and wags his tail faster. He realises it, he feels it, it is possible to live here. It would be easy to get used to walking a couple of kilometres to buy bread until you blend into the local landscape without attracting attention. Or to digest food under a roof of dried palm branches as a pair of white and black hands slide over a backgammon board. Or throw a fishing line into the sand as it's forbidden to throw it into the sea. You arch your body forward and backwards until you reach a harmonious point of tai chi. It's perfect: you already know that you won't catch anything, the tip of the hook will fly and only remove a few grains of stupefied sand. The only objective is the beauty of the movement, the balancing equilibrium.

Then I approach another fear which begins to grow. What would happen if life became a succession of sunny and rainy days in different scenarios? What if there is no turning back? What would happen if we stopped trying to control everything that happens in our lives?

It's not cold, but I shudder when I return to my Sudanese friends with thoughts of selling the remains of my past life and surrendering to the road and Alzheimer's. There's Anna, Adam, Umniya, Winnie, Jorick, Taf Taf, Tyson, Adel, Yasir and Jafar. Jafar's skin is so intensely black the only thing you can see of him at night is his smile. I sit on a cushion next to Adam, who tells stories of his tribe.

"I'm a Bagghara. Bagghara means cows. In my tribe there's more cows than people. Everyone has cows and they move them from one place to the other to graze. My family has 400 cows and we move around by riding them. Our tradition is so deep-rooted with raising cows that before we get married we need to pass a test: we have to ride a wild cow and hold on until the future father-in-law says it's enough. It's very important because if you fall off he can forbid the wedding."

"And you fell? I mean, you're not married."

"No, I didn't fall or find a wife," he replies lowering his gaze, uncomfortably.

No man in Sudan is completely a man if he doesn't have a wife and sons. Adam is already 44 years old, too old. In this land, he could be a grandfather, or dead.

"Twelve years ago I was about to marry," he continues slowly. He struggles to speak, his grief becomes physical, but he continues in a conscious effort to overcome the discomfort. "Everything was ready, but at the last minute she said that we should go live with her family. I told her that this could not be, I wanted to work the lands of my family, like all Sudanese men, not those of her father. So we never married. A few years ago I met an Italian woman that wanted to marry me. There are tourists that arrive and a week later they marry a Bedouin or a Black African like me; they like us because it's very romantic and adventurous. But the Italian didn't want to have children."

Adam would like to have a wife. He had many opportunities to sign a marriage contract for a week; a special privilege for those practising Muslims who would only bed a woman after a wedding.

Life is easy at Nuweiba Beach with Adam, Jorick, Winnie and Umniya

But he wants a woman that will stick around, not one that's passing through. He's not interested in sexual tourism. The last time he called home, two- and-a-half years ago, his mother asked him the name of his wife and how many children he had. Since then he has not called his family.

Under the open roof of the hut there is space for eight groups, eight fires, but only one brightens the cement walls decorated with black bodies dancing and lists of prices in misspelt English. Everyone was counting on October, the month of Jewish holidays. But in October the undeclared war between Israel and Palestine continued. If tourists don't come, there's no money.

At that point solidarity starts to work. Those with savings buy food for everyone. Working in Cairo makes no sense: they would earn 100 or 150 Egyptian pounds a month, which they'd spend on lodging and food. It's better to stay here, and wait for April, for some accidental tourist. Wait, and everything will change, *inshallah*. Wait. The warmth of the brothers at the beach is better than the cold anonymity of the city.

In the light of the fire, I look around at the faces. Everyone wants to return to Sudan, nobody dreams of dying in Egypt or in any other country of the world. But if they return to their land with empty hands, why did they leave? Returning without money is a matter of shame, even though half of what they earn is sent back to their families.

Adel's objective is to live in London. Last summer he was determined to save at least 3,000 Egyptian pounds. He managed to save 7,000. But at the end of the season his best friend died tragically in a traffic accident and, as custom dictates, the Sudanese from Nuweiba raised money to send to the family of the deceased. That's the African life insurance policy. He sent 3,000 pounds. He sent 2,000 to his own family, he gave 1,000 to help out a friend who ended up in prison. The last 1,000 disappeared in expenses and small loans that cannot be denied. Loaned money is almost never returned and only grants the right to ask when things go badly for you. Sometimes life is a dog that chases its own tail.

New faces arrive constantly and, after greeting us with a *salaam aleikum,* they sit on the coloured strips of rug which separate us from the sand. Yasir moves to my side, it's his turn to tell a story. Then another man appears, a mute, and everyone greets him warmly. In the Arab world, mutes, the blind, the deaf, those crippled or paralysed, all disabled people are treated with special love.

What happens next is extraordinary.

The mute begins to speak and everyone listens to him. The monotone sound that leaves his throat is the accent to the drawings he traces with his hands, either on the sand or in the air. Sometimes he needs to repeat something, either a gesture or a guttural sound. But no one tires or becomes impatient while listening to him. Nobody ignores him.

On the straw wall, the shadow of Yafar repeats Yafar's movement: he lifts the teapot, fills the shadow cups, pretends to drink. Everyone laughs adding truth to the legend that the Sudanese are always laughing. The mute speaks, opens his mouth to let loose a silent laugh, he explains his news and even wins the contest for the biggest liar of the night, when he promises to get the necessary permits to take us on a journey to the centre of the earth.

When they found Suleyman hanging, swinging like a scarecrow on a lonely tree in the Sinai desert, police suspected it was related to a settling of accounts. It was an honour killing.

The rumour grew slowly. As the days passed someone heard something, neighbours noticed an absence, women wove plots in the corners and men assumed the law at bar tables. It was unfair because they were young, but it was the law. Even the elders remembered the sentence they had heard from their own grandparents: love is not free.

Suleyman was in love with a woman from another family and she loved him back. But he had not followed the steps tradition dictates: he had not asked for her hand from her father or even asked permission to see her. An unwritten law sentenced Suleyman for robbery. He had taken the daughter of Mustafa without paying a dowry. He had stolen. The good name and honour of Mustafa's family had been violated and had to be restored.

The old law, tradition, remains unappeasable in these corners of the desert. Fifteen virgin girls are given away in matrimony by a Pakistani tribe in compensation for a wave of murders that began with the death of a donkey. A beautiful young girl is beaten to death by her husband so she'll stop drawing the attention of the neighbours. Another woman is imprisoned in Iran for walking down the street with a man who is not from her family. A woman has sulphuric acid thrown in her face in retaliation for something. Suleyman was executed when he was 20 years old.

For her, despised by her people and her family for having broken the rules, a crueller fate was expected. Because she was no longer a virgin, her father would marry her off to an older man, a widower or someone elderly, or become the fourth and last wife of a rich man.

In the name of honour, a year later someone close to Suleyman would end the life of one of the children or siblings of the murderer who had escaped to some remote location in the mountains. On the second anniversary there would be another death to avenge the death from the previous year, insuring a series of annual murders for the next 20 to 30 years. A son for a son, a brother for a brother, a relative for a relative. Then no one would remember the reasons for so much blood, or that the honour had been broken because of a love story.

I keep thinking about this Arabic version of Romeo and Juliet when we arrive at the Monastery of St. Catherine, at the foot of Mount Sinai. It was built when English and Spanish were still dialects, and the word America didn't exist, it didn't mean anything. The enormous blocks of stone of the outer walls, funded by the religious fervour of a Byzantine emperor, are the walls of a fortress. The windows, open for the last two thousand years, are crossed by old iron bars, and are square, rectangular and semicircular. There is at least one for every historic epoch.

Inside there's still a small community of orthodox Christian monks who guard the certificate of safe conduct which Mohammed, the prophet of Islam, gave them in the seventh century. It saved them from the Arabic avalanche that conquered all of North Africa. Almost 1,500 years later the monks survive off the sale of postcards and miniature replicas of the holy mountain.

Today it's another beautiful afternoon, blue, bright and clear. The same as yesterday: *play yesterday's weather forecast and no one would know the difference.*

There is no wind or storms on the horizon and the trees planted by the side of the road survive with the help of gardeners wearing turbans. Three huge buses leave the parking lot with their cargo of docile tourists, pilgrims with some excursionist bible under their arm.

"Three thousand steps carved by hand! If the guide says so it must be true, *oui oui*," repeats a retired Frenchwoman.

Near the door, a group of elderly women in a trance and youths armed with guitars destroy the sanctity of the monastery. According to the Old Testament, Jehovah gave the tablets of the Ten Commandments to Moses, the patriarch of the Jews, Christians and Muslims, on a nearby hill.

"It takes two hours to climb, and it's hot, very hot," explain four Bedouins engaged in the age-old business of renting out camels. "Very hot-hot."

When they finally understand that we would prefer to walk, they show us a postcard they received from Japan. They want us to read it aloud. Some of these men speak some English, but translating these written words into sound is much more difficult

"Dear Saleh. Thanks for your friendship. That was the first mountain I have ever climbed in my life and I still remember the lovely hours I spent sitting on your camel. How is your family?"

While Anna reads, more Bedouins come closer to listen to the news from Tokyo. Everyone smiles, it's impossible not to be infected by the joy that fills the air. Those who understand English translate it to those who have forgotten about the sale of trinkets and rent-a-camel. This is far more interesting. A man with a horrible scar in place of his upper lip laughs and shows his gums through his missing teeth. When Anna finishes, Saleh takes up a pen and paper.

"Writing letter for friend?"

"Alright..." replies Anna. "What would you like to say?"

"I don't know... here we are good, how is her family. Tell her to come back..."

"How would you like to start? *'Dear Misoko'*, is that alright?"

"Yes, yes, very good," reply other voices. The letter is becoming a collective statement.

"*'Dear Misoko, how are you? How is your family? I hope everyone at home is doing well.'* Is that alright?"

"Yes, yes."

"What else?"

"I hope she comes back soon."

Behind Saleh there is some suppressed laughter. The circle closes in a bit and as Anna draws Western hieroglyphics the crowd murmurs approvingly.

"*'It has snowed on top of our mountains and there are few tourists because of the war between the Israelis and the Palestinians. The camels are well and we continue going to the top of Mount Sinai every day.'* Okay?"

"Very okay."

"*'I miss you and I hope your next letter will be saying that you will return soon.'* Did you marry her Saleh?" asks Anna suddenly, amidst laughter which reaches as far as her words, running from mouth to mouth to those furthest away.

"Nooooo," replies Saleh, his face red with embarrassment, rejecting categorically having united both extremes of Asia in a bed.

His companions launch barbs at him in Arabic, in a second everyone has lost their innocence. With a quick gesture he raises his hand to quell the noise, but a few continue to laugh.

"What else? Do you want me to write *habibi,* at the end of the letter?" asks Anna.

"Yes, *habibi,* very good."

Who knows if he will ever see Misoko again. Inshallah. At the moment the only important thing is the fulfilled promise, that piece of coloured Japanese cardboard with a reproduction of a symmetrical snow-covered mountain on it. Another sacred mountain. In Arab countries the future is in the hands of Allah. And today is a beautiful day, blue, bright and clear.

" *'With much love to my habibi, Saleh.'* "

Asia finishes in a white tunnel, overly lit, overly like the stifling narrowness described by those who have been at the threshold of death and have returned to tell about it. The tunnel, as short as the memories of new-borns, passes under the Suez Canal and flows into the light. Finally, Africa.

Nothing changes on the other side, however. There's still the same beat-up cars, the same olive-coloured faces, the same dust in the air, the same unforgettable heat.

The most effective mechanism of discovery is the mistake. You become famous for a well interpreted catastrophic failure. You're a biologist, you intentionally get lost in a distant and remote forest, and you find a smelly pond filled with six-legged frogs. You ramble around aimlessly through the city when your feet take you to a medieval alley that was never there before. Perhaps that's why we're followed by a silent ambulance of the Red Crescent through the jumbled streets of Suez. In broken English they ask us, *please, mister,* leave this neighbourhood immediately: this is an Islamist Bronx.

We follow a line of insignificant ants across the desert on a thin grey line and we sleep behind the embankment of the railroad tracks. Sterile fields again shelter us under a dark and silent cloak, warmed by stars. A few minutes after two in the morning a cargo train passes, loud and sombre, endless, that awakens memories of run-away camels, of ancient dead who unsheathed their scimitars in a single motion and lie forever between us. The hostilities start the following morning while we add ourselves to the schizophrenic flow of Cairo.

As we join the traffic, an interesting and implacable sense begins to grow within us: no one cares about anything. Bicycles, pedestrians, camels, donkey carts and street sellers survive being run down on the same piece of asphalt. All trucks, cars and buses display some scar; they're fighting animals, and they're all male.

There is a van with a broken axle abandoned in the middle of the street, a car about to fall into one of the canals of the Nile, and another ambulance, this time with desperate sirens wailing, waiting for two drivers to finish unravelling the meaning of life. Minibuses continue circulating on the streets at their own pace. They shout their destiny, braking suddenly in front of anyone who lifts a hand, even if the movement was actually intended to swat a fly. Then they incorporate them- selves into the insane blind waltz of the street, creating a sharp chorus of horns, brakes and violent shouting; a school of wild children with new trumpets. If they have to go right, they'll turn into traffic even if they're in the most distant left lane. In a terrifying instant, filthy and arrogant trucks leave no doubt about who is in charge. Traffic lights either don't work or serve no purpose; in every corner there is one, two or four policemen who are in charge of complicating the flow of traffic more, or much more, depending on their skills.

After a few kilometres, and with my nerves to the point of becoming fried spaghetti, I give Anna the dubious privilege of driving in this exaggerated Neapolitan chaos. We're looking for a campsite that's located (and it couldn't possibly be any other way) on the other side of town.

The Overlander mythology has always enlarged Cairo, and amid the groups of people who gather in the corners of bars to plan trips across Africa, the dangers of these streets always come up. There are stories of foreign all-terrain vehicles which lost their wheels within two minutes and find themselves sitting on brick crutches. There are Stories of broken windows, or expertly dismantled vans with forced locks and interiors gutted by a storm of swirling arms. Stories of handbags cut with a surgical precision that could split a hair lengthwise. It's the work of professionals, people who excel in their trade.

It was a good enough reason to let ourselves be drawn through the tide of Cairo with caution. On the sidewalks people bump calmly into one another but don't stop, it's a constant sinuous movement that repels men and women. Clothes are deformed and rubbed in an inconsistent cadence. If someone lifts an arm, the galabiya have wings. The air of Giza, rarefied by a thick cloud of grey pollution, barely allows a glimpse at the spectacle that waits at the end of the Avenue of the Pyramids. Triangles, giant triangles.

Suddenly a young man breaks the choreography and starts shouting from the sidewalk. He's short, perhaps only a metre sixty, thin, with black hair and thick moustache. Strangest of all, he's yelling at us. Another mistake, we don't know anyone here, actually, we don't know anyone in all Africa. I give him a papal-style wave, raising my hand and shaking it gently without moving my elbow as I have learned in recent months. I smile coolly and beatifically. The traffic, slow and heavy because of a truck that's difficult to digest, is stopped at a traffic light. I'm not too sure where this campsite is found, and I'm wondering if we'll arrive anywhere today. Then I see that this fellow is running towards us in the middle of the street, dodging side mirrors with the agility of a centre forward soccer player before stopping at our window.

"Where are you going?"

"We're looking for the Harraneia campground."

"I know it. I can guide you there," he says while opening the door and gesticulating with his hands for me to make room, seating himself almost on my knees. "My name is Samir and I know the owner, don't worry. Where are you from?"

I turn my head and look at him, now I have my neck twisted against the roof. Samir laughs, sitting up straight on my seat. He's probably more comfortable than in any of the passenger minibuses. Anna continues driving and every brake, every pot-hole, every speed bump, breaks new limits with regards to the flexibility of my neck. *Oy!* A few minutes later Samir invites us to his house, a few days ago some Belgians stayed with him.

"Jorick, Winnie and Bosra?"

"They had a dog," he continues without listening.

"Yes, Bosra, they found him in Syria."

"Do you know them?"

Among the millions of people that live in Cairo, we have crossed paths with the one who sheltered our friends and their Land Rover with demonic plates. It's incredible, one person out of eighteen million, a coincidence as improbable as winning the lottery. All of my initial fears dissipate quickly, though we don't know if our friends are still alive or buried in the desert.

We leave the road thirty kilometres to the south. We cross another canal with dense Nile water and we slip through the labyrinth of streets and mud houses. I don't read lips, much less in Arabic, but we must be getting close. The neighbours' faces show the tips of their noses and express the same thing: *that demented Samir has brought more strangers back home.*

"Welcome to Abu Sir!"

We park the van in an alley and walk a hundred metres through narrow passages of uneven ground to an old adobe brick house. Just as we walk into the door, Fregha appears. His wife is short, has the large round face of a young girl, and sighs theatrically. To the right is a small room, crammed with carpets and maroon cushions. A few steps further is a small open courtyard, a bathroom and a staircase that leads to the overhead bedroom. To the left there's a dark kitchen, with white walls covered in simple drawings, childlike, done in charcoals: a girl holds the reins of a camel, a mosque surrounded by palm trees, a square house, a daisy against a pyramid.

Samir is an energetic sort who seems to constantly live in a state of tense friendliness; a sort of boy scout always ready to go outside or solve a problem. His favourite sport is talking: he's thirty-seven years old and his wife is twenty-eight, his mother is currently on her way home after making the *hajj,* the pilgrimage to Mecca that all good Muslims must make at least once in their life. That he has two children and that's enough. That when he found us, he had just finished work at the Pyramid Hospital. That he's a security guard. That many foreigners have passed through his house, that all they had to do is to leave a written message in his guestbook. That a New Zealander once stayed twenty-two days. That another girl ran out of money, he lent her five hundred dollars and her family returned it by mail. That a German with a Syrian father had returned twice. That we're to make ourselves at home and that we can stay as long as we like.

"Come along, let's bring the cattle home from the fields," he states at the first awkward silence. There are still a couple of hours left in another day of fasting.

Despite his stature, he walks with long, quick, agile and nervous steps. Interestingly, he's the first Arab I've seen who seems in a hurry. His face, hard and dark, softens a bit when greeting neighbours who see us walk through the village towards the parcel of land where his family cultivates alfalfa.

Yellow does not exist in the fields, everything is a fluorescent green, an anxious green excited to germinate in one of the few narrow fertile ribbons which cross the Sahara. On each side there are narrow islands of thin palm trees loaded with dates, and groups of *fellahin,* farmers of the Nile, that drop their hoes and raise their arms. The greeting is not an obligation, the happiness of seeing a foreigner crossing their fields is genuine.

By exactly five o'clock all the animals have been gathered into their stables: the donkey, the ox, the cow with her calf and two goats occupy a room on the ground floor of Samir's mother's house. The streets are empty; Ramadan is the time of the year when sunsets are most celebrated. Everyone waits for the song of the muezzin announcing the fast is over today.

Minutes later Fregha enters the dining room with an enormous tray balanced on her head and a pot of tea in each hand. It's the private show of a juggling housewife. There are plates with salads, chicken soup, rice, bread, stuffed vegetables and potatoes in tomato sauce. After the last bite, Samir sighs with satisfaction. He claps his hands in the air, he washes them in a bowl of water and begins to prepare a narghile. He hasn't smoked today either.

That night, after hours of slamming dominoes down on a table under the thick cloud of smoke at a neighbourhood coffee shop, another dinner before bed, more conversation, tea and sweet tobacco, Samir affirms that we're not just his friends. We're also not just his guests. We are his brothers. He leads us to our room – his bedroom.

Very little has changed in Abu Sir since the time of the pharaohs. The village remains a maze of twisting alleys and worn adobe walls. The houses are occupied by large women, hyperactive children and moustached men who wear long garments, like their great-grandfathers before them. Everyone dreams of owning a pick-up taxi to go to the city loaded with people, but in real life they settle for a donkey. Yes, there are some telephones, many televisions and lots of radio cassette players that turn the streets into a remix of prayers to Allah and Egyptian pop music, but that's only the make-up that hides the traditional course of the Nile.

Children grow up splitting their time in school with hours of work. They herd animals, stack merchandise and shout in the markets. During their free afternoons, they chase balls in barren desert fields or run about the tombstones of the cemetery, where families meet every Friday to have lunch with their dead. They also have coloured toys, weapons to kill invisible Zionists and cars that only a cockroach could drive. But when they climb the barren hills on the outskirts of Abu Sir they have fun raising a plastic bag tied to the tip of a stick. If the wind is favourable, we have a new flag of freedom.

Women show their faces, ankles and hands while they walk with buckets of water delicately balanced on their heads. Some of them carry enormous bundles of freshly cut grass for animals that remain at home today. Others carry clothes or wet carpets they have just finished washing at the banks of the canal. Their red, blue or purple dresses contrast with the white walls painted with naive drawings. There are planes, boats, buses and representations of the Kaaba, the holiest site of Islam, at Mecca. They are on the houses of the faithful who have completed the *hajj*.

At dusk the streets empty and become slowly streaked with yellow, lit by bare bulbs from shops that stay open until the seller falls asleep. From the roofs there is desperate meowing and crowing, cats compete with roosters for ownership of hens. Afterwards the first meal and the first narghile of the day, the streets fill up again.

At 7 pm, however, the streets empty again. Every television in the village is focused on the misadventures of Mansur, the protagonist in the most popular soap opera of this part of the world. Traders rely on the honesty of their neighbours and neglect business to concentrate on the screen. Women are always at home and men stop playing noisy games of domino to turn their chairs around and concentrate on today's episode. Can Mansur overcome his base instincts and behave like a decent man? Will he stop getting into trouble and deceiving his friends? Will he be able to run his life properly and bring happiness to his family as a good Muslim should?

Apart from fasting and the adventures of Mansur, in Abu Sir nothing seems too important. The pyramids of the Fifth Dynasty which rise on the horizon have seen many generations born, mourn, laugh and die. They saw a 25-year-old Samir go to a party with a rehearsed speech to say to Fregha: *Marry me.*

They had spoken little, men and women don't mix unless they are from the same family, but they liked what they saw. He was a good Muslim, practised Karate and had muscles of steel. She was pretty, had a mischievous smile and laughed a lot. He said everything he expected of her, and unlike other men, he only wanted to have one wife. She laughed again and accepted.

A few days later Samir's father knocked on the door of Fregha's family home. He had something important to settle with the man of the house. They sat facing each other separated by a low table. They drank tea and ate cakes covered in syrup, spoke proudly of their lives and their businesses, smoked narghile and settled the dowry. She was a respected girl, well educated, and knew how to do many things. But this time there was also love, so her father asked for a reasonable dowry.

Months later they married. She soon became pregnant and had a son, a blessing from Allah. Samir bought an old house in the middle of the narrow maze in Abu Sir and after a while stopped raising chickens. The cats were too smart. Five years later their first daughter arrived. As their children began to grow up they started to sleep at his widowed mother's house, until they permanently settled there. Now they sleep with their cousins, surrounded by animals and a lot of dusty dirt roads. For a child, this must be happiness.

Today Fregha is fuller and has a less innocent smile. She is not convinced with her husband's hospitality; it means more work for her. Samir doesn't care, the rules say he works in town and she works at home. Meals have to be ready, on time, and must be abundant. Afterwards she has to serve two rounds of tea. If she needs money to buy food, he has to give it to her. Then she gives back the change; men are responsible for finances. If he's out of tobacco, Samir will ask her to go to the store. If there are any children around, she will send them for it.

Another evening of tea, narghile and Egyptian music after another day of fasting, a curious nephew of about 16 or 17 shows up. He looks for a large cushion and sits next to me. It's the best place to observe gestures, to travel to faraway places without leaving Abu Sir. We represent a living chapter on the subject of Western customs, something right out of National Geographic.

He barely speaks, he's only there to observe. Samir inserts another cassette with catchy rhythms, it's not raï, it's not Sufi, it's pop. The narghile goes around and without realising what I'm doing, I pass the pipe to Curious Nephew. Suddenly Fregha stirs uncomfortably and throws sharp glances at Samir and the boy and an icy silence descends on the room. Something's not right.

Curious Nephew inhales and lets out satisfied clouds of minty smoke. He knows he's just broken an unwritten law; smoking before an adult means he's become a man. He's just moved above Fregha's status, and she's furious.

This act of shamelessness only costs him a reprimand at the door of the house. But the damage has been done, he's now an equal. Curious Nephew is happy.

★

The preparations for celebrating the end of Ramadan increase the workload for women. Tradition dictates that everything should be bright for the festivities of Eid al-Fitr, and everything means everything: carpets, clothes, furniture, mattresses, sheets, cushions, cushion covers, lamps, curtains and the dark corners of the kitchen. The floor needs to be scrubbed on hands and knees and the walls must be washed with a soapy sponge. Vehicles, children and donkeys have to shine. Everyone wears a new galabiya and buys gifts for children. Consumption soars as much as during the Christian Christmas. It's a spectacular marketing success.

Shops work overtime and everyone hurries to get home. A huge feast must be prepared, emotions grow and spread as the day progresses. It's the exaltation of something extraordinary, the end of thirst and hunger, the end of the month in which the prophet Mohammed received the first revelation of the Qur'an. The end of Ramadan approaches.

Fregha runs, the floor is flooded with foam, the house shakes itself dry. When she opens the door to the bath to fill another bucket of water, she discovers Anna putting on her new orange galabiya with golden ribbons. She's surprised but she wants to see if what they say in town is true. She wants to know if Western women don't completely shave their pubic hair.

In the salon, Samir proudly inspects my new white galabiya. This is one of the best nights of the year, everything must be well prepared, perfect. He places the white *keffiyeh* on my head with both hands. He smiles and steps back to look me over.

"There's still something missing brother. You have too much hair on your head."

I tremble, but I manage to get the local barber to only trim my beard. His oval mirror reflects a familiar face. Everything else is new, it had never happened before. Is it possible to know how I arrived here, to an unknown village on the banks of the Nile, to celebrate the end of a month of fasting for Ramadan, dressed like an Arab?

A year-and-a-half ago I used to live in my office, are we living in Africa? Who is this guy looking at me with my face?

So far the trip has been a succession of warm days, a permanent spring with only a couple of showers. Will it continue to be the same? Will it always be a one-way trip? The barber, who is probably also a mechanic, has a collection of damaged pistons next to his shaving knives.

★

The next morning, too early to believe that we've been partying last night, *warm beer, shots or firecrackers in the street, a special blend with hemp for the narghile, and I think, what a headache,* I again dress with my white galabiya and go with Samir to the first prayer of the year.

It's still not daybreak and the loud speakers on the mosques remind everyone that it's better to pray than to sleep, but I'm not so sure.

When we leave the last street of Abu Sir the scene is overwhelming. About 3,000 men dressed in pure white line up on the sand like an army of faith. Samir runs towards them while I climb up a promontory. The first words of the imam who leads the pray are pushed by the wind of the coming dawn. The answer is a sweeping proclamation.

"There is no god but God and Mohammed is his prophet."

Unlike Christianity, Islam is not limited to occupying a place in society's memory. It has as much influence on daily life as the Catholic Church did in Europe a hundred years ago. It calls people to pray five times a day through powerful speakers, it has a say and a vote on the nature of relations between men and women, it calls for fasting during daylight hours for 30 days a year and it mobilises massive pilgrimages.

In the Arab world faith still influences state politics. Extremism is only one facet embraced by a minority and highlighted by the media for its unbridled violence.

"There is no god but God and Mohammed is his prophet."

While men get up and then prostrate themselves again in the direction of the first rays of sun, women remain seated on the tombs of the cemetery. They wait and watch over children who shout, play and dirty their bright new clothes.

"There is no god but God and Mohammed is his prophet."

The vast majority of Muslims treat visitors like brothers from another faith. For them, the important thing is to believe, to have only one god, a single Allah, call him what you will. We Christians are the People of the Book, the People of the New Testament.

When prayers end, all the men embrace one another for long moments. Today is Eid al-Fitr, the festivity of the end of Ramadan and the streets are filled with joy. Everyone, known or unknown, greets and repeats *"yiunaam untataibi"* to wish happiness.

After the first daylight narghile in quite some time, we visit Samir's mother, a small, wrinkled old woman who permanently dresses in

Greetings at the outskirts of Abu Sir at the end of Ramadan

black. She belongs to a class of mothers who are kind and resilient, survivors who have tasted a teaspoon full of the syrup of immortality. Women who never die, who just shrink a bit year after year until one day they suddenly disappear.

The grandmother has just returned from Mecca with presents for the family, neighbours and unexpected visitors. She takes us to her kitchen and gives us a Muslim rosary of white beads linked by a green cord; the Saudi colours.

In the salon, men and women sit in two separate groups. The walls of the house are of exposed brick and the floors are bare concrete with carpets in the inhabited quarters: around the narghile, in the bedrooms, and in the television room. Mohammed, Samir's brother, turns on a radio cassette player that makes more noise than the cow, who is mournfully mooing because she won't be going out to pasture today. Samir translates the conversations from Arabic into English and back into Arabic, and between jokes and laughter, his children go off to buy tobacco, collect the empty glasses of tea and bring what is asked of them. It's the price they must pay to learn the gestures of grown-ups.

When someone arrives they're offered the place of honour, the most comfortable, closest to the narghile. The expanding circle of men grows and the women, including Anna, retire to a far corner.

That night, the last in Abu Sir, we pay a visit that is far from routine. At the end of a narrow road flanked by palm trees there is another village on the banks of the Nile.

"Would you like to see some mummies?" a relative of Samir had asked that afternoon.

The *mummies* are a Coptic sculpture and a simple representation of Tutankhamen carved in volcanic rock. It could be any Pharaoh, but Tutankhamen is the most famous one. The starting price is 2,000 dollars.

Trafficking in antiquities could solve a few economic problems. But to get into this game you have to know about mummies and know that you're risking your neck. Egyptian prisons are not very welcoming.

"The desert is full of tombs," explains Samir. "It's forbidden to dig, but people are always looking and sometimes they even find something.

They drive in the dark to some remote site, and while some watch, others dig and others prepare a narghile. Just before sunrise they return home with empty hands or some new decoration for the back room."

★

After the truce marked by Ramadan, the mosquitos return in hungry droves. Anna awakens on the day we have decided to continue with our trip with sixteen bites on one side of her face. She looks like she's just gone through a tribal scarification ritual. We dedicate the rest of the morning to buying fruits, vegetables, moist tobacco and a small narghile which is added to our permanent baggage. We fill up both fuel tanks with a hundred and thirty litres of diesel and, just before we're about to leave, Samir offers us four round breads, thin, hard and crunchy, the size of a large pizza.

"For the desert," he explains. "This bread will keep for weeks, many weeks. It's eaten hard, but you can also soften it by sprinkling it with a bit of water."

At that moment the emotions associated with our destiny, always leaving, return. Always leaving, never staying.

"Brother," he continues a few moments later, "you know that my house is your house. Come back whenever you like."

Sahara means desert, an empty place where there's nothing, though that's not exactly true either. The slight vegetation of the oasis allows the existence of small animals, foxes, scorpions, snakes and birds who only leave their hiding places when the sunsets. The larger mammals, leopards, cheetahs, oryx, antelopes and hyenas survive only in the illustrations of old books.

Long caravans of camels still traverse the sand dunes of the Sahara. They walk from the north of Sudan towards Cairo through 1,000 miles of barren landscapes that would make anyone think they were crossing limbo. Their guides, shepherds as black as the blackest night, out of place amid the light brown faces of Cairo, are simple souls, thin people whose smiles belie the difficulty of their work. The animals are relatively lucky; they don't have to haul the weight of the goods that now travel by truck. Apart from the water they'll need for the journey, they only have to take their own flesh to the slaughterhouse.

Unlike the hard and motionless fields of Syria and Jordan, North Africa's travelling dunes move grain by grain with the hot breath of the wind. On each side of the road, sand mixes with small stones in lonely landscapes without limit or end, as broad and boundless as a vacuum. The desolation, beautiful, unfolds stubbornly before disappearing over the horizon. Nothing can be hidden when there are no obstacles in sight. It's a body in a catatonic state that hardly blinks under almost 40 degrees Celsius in the shade. Winter has just begun.

Amid this harsh universe flourishes Bawiti, the most important town in the oasis of Bahariyya. After 340 kilometres, just over a centimetre on the map, yet so much desert, the first houses surrounded by palm trees seem to appear like mirages. They're basic cubes made of mud bricks covered with plaster painted in colours and doors crowned by Arabic numerals drawn by hand. At the edge of town a bunch of children abandon their swings to jump and shake their arms. *Look, a car!* I push the button to the auxiliary horn that mimics the sound of mooing and their hands become frozen in the air. *Where's the cow?*

Any house on the main street could be one of those stores that stock not more than 20 or 30 different products, less than you would find in your kitchen cabinets. All of them offer rice, pasta, sugar and loose tea, soap, cans of sardines and vegetable oil. Some have powdered milk, others dates and the furthest ones have olive oil and cans of beans used to prepare ful. There are restaurants for passengers beside the road and food stalls for locals between the lonely streets of the town. We have *kushari* for lunch, rice with chopped up spaghetti, lentils and chickpeas, all mixed up, and we pass some time smoking a narghile in a coffee shop, just off the main street. Then the wind starts to blow.

First, there are unexpected bursts which leave us shivering. Then, a thin white cloud arrives, a low cloud, a whirlwind of flying dust which starts to load up our pockets. When the wind becomes confident, the chairs walk on their own, the corrugated iron roofs rattle out of time and the galabiyas, runaways, move one metre in front or behind their owner. At any moment we'll have an Arab imitating Marilyn Monroe.

On the sidewalk, the vegetable vendors hide inside their clothes to protect themselves from the sandstorm. Heads of lettuce gain weight and a Black boy with curly hair becomes white faster than Michael Jackson. Traffic stops, houses disappear and the kerbs become covered with thin sand that flies and perversely attacks the skin like needles. The streets empty.

Half an hour later the wind disappears as quickly as it arrived. After a final whirl, the sand stops, relaxes. The village is covered with a layer of cream filling every hole in the asphalt and smoothing all the edges. Then, people return to the street.

When the stores reopen we look for bread, beer and red meat to celebrate our first New Year's Eve in the desert. We only find bread. Cold beer mutates into orange-flavoured Mirinda and the red meat becomes a live chicken which we hand-pick, *that one, the white one with yellow eyes*. One minute later it's slaughtered and plucked using a manual centrifuge that looks like a washing machine.

Before sunset we leave the road heading west, to Libya. There's no path, but that doesn't matter, the soil is hard. We park next to a volcanic cone of black rocks that jingle like glass, and start preparing the feast. We have to remove the last of the feathers on the chicken and light a fire with the wood we picked up in the oasis. The sky changes colour and the last rays of sunlight reflect on one aspiring cloud. But no, this is the Sahara, it doesn't rain here.

We inhale the first sweet puffs on the new narghile while small potatoes cook on the coals. Four aubergines complain on the grill bought in Jordan, and a fox sits patiently waiting some fifteen metres away. Some chicken will fall. We uncork the bottle of Mirinda and we intoxicate ourselves on dozens of shooting stars, comets willing to commit suicide to supplement the beauty of our first New Year's Eve away from Santa Claus and his gang. From the foot of our volcano our desert unfolds, illuminated by a Muslim crescent moon, thin, new, independent.

★

The next day we cross the Farafra Oasis and continue to Dakhla. Another green island of houses and foliage recedes in the distance and the desert wins again. Towards the east rises a plateau which appears committed to join the trip. It immovably sits forty metres above the road and keeps charge over us.

Tens of metres below us there is water, an underground subterranean ocean, but up here everything is dead. A dried tumbleweed rolls restlessly and unpredictably, stopping in the other lane. As well as stones, there are rabbit droppings, footprints of foxes and lizards, but I don't see any rabbits, foxes or lizards. There are only streaks of sand that run across the road on their way to another dune.

We cross ancient caravan stops now converted into blistering hot villages, with streets designed like mud tunnels to avoid the sweltering heat of the sun and the violence of the sandstorms. But no one lives here, there are only stray dogs and herds of children playing hide-and-seek who appear sporadically at the end of the long and dusty passages. One second later they have disappeared. Perhaps they were never there.

Some houses have lost their doors but still retain their lintel of hard-as-rock wood engraved with Arabic inscriptions. On the walls are giant postmarks done in red or blue paint remembering ancient pilgrimages to Mecca. The houses, well under way in their inevitable process of decomposition, have windows open or missing, and are distressingly empty. Maybe they're just listening. The inhabitants moved to the suburbs and built new neighbourhoods of brick. The heart of the old village is a ghost town.

At the entrance to Kharga, the largest oasis in western Egypt, we're stopped by a barricade at a police road check. They salute courteously, write down the number of our Egyptian license plate, two Spaniards and our destination: Kharga, Paris, Luxor.

"Are you going to sleep in Kharga?"

"I don't know."

"Where will you be tomorrow?"

"I don't know. Perhaps in Kharga, perhaps further south, in Paris. I don't know."

Policemen don't like imprecision. The controls are justified as a protection against the spread of Islamic fundamentalism, but I never really feel in danger. It's true, we did witness the start of a few fights and during the last night of Ramadan some fellow tried to start something up with me. "What are you looking at?" he asked with wild eyes when he noticed I was watching him.

I ignored him and nothing happened. That was on the outskirts of Cairo, but people here are friendly and curious. Just like these police officers. After they wave us on, they rush to their truck with all the official coloured lights, and give us a police escort into the city. I don't know if they're bored or if they just want to protect us.

"Now what?" I ask Anna.

"I don't know, we can't exactly tell them to go away. We don't want a police escort."

We always prefer to get lost in the streets and find what we're after on our own, even though that's more complicated. But here, authorities do not want to risk appearing in the papers. We can't simply say "goodbye, no thanks."

"Tour guides," says Anna.

"What?"

"They can be our tour guides. If they insist on accompanying us we can't do anything about that. We'll simply go to all the places we intended to go. All of them, including those which we hadn't intended on visiting," she says with an evil twinkle in her eye.

First, we visit the magnificent Temple of Hibis where the grounds-keeper, on seeing the police escort, assumes we're important visitors. Then, he opens the gates which separate the common tourist from the low reliefs which still conserve their original colours so we can study them in detail. From there, we go to an eatery and have a meal of *ful*, fries and salad. After that we go find a place to smoke an apple-flavoured narghile, by invitation of The Authorities. Today is another holiday Friday, but we still need to go to the market: bananas, oranges, melons, and three police officers to help us carry the shopping bags. I start feeling somewhat important. We leave everything in the van, and I show them the burnt-out light bulb of an old flashlight. I leave the hardest thing for last: refilling our small kitchen cylinder with propane.

Despite the impassive smile, The Authorities are starting to get tired. After another hour of to-ing and fro-ing in the suburbs, we find Mr. Propane Man, relaxing in a coffee shop on his day off. At my sign of triumph, the two armed policemen who travel in the back of the escort truck raise their fists in victory. We've done it.

"And now, you're going to Paris?" they ask smiling. They're tired of travelling around the empty streets with us and all they want to do is leave us at the start of the desert, where their authority ends. And if it's possible, for the Fundamentalists to kill us.

"Now Paris."

They set aside their rifles and start singing and clapping hands with real joy, like children.

★

Paris or Baris, the Arabs pronounce all their "P's" like a "B," is a border town of about two thousand people. It's quiet, nothing happens there, nothing ever happens. There are some ancient burial stones to which nobody pays attention, and a small oasis surrounded by an ocean of sand which produces just enough for its inhabitants not to die of starvation or scurvy. Paris or Baris, is loneliness, isolation and survival on an island faraway from all trade routes. Paris or Baris, Sahara, is remote.

After the village, further on, there are few signs of life. The desert besieges the people and only desperate settlers, or Bedouins, dare settle themselves around the few water wells further south to Ash Shabb and Sudan. We know the possibility of using the road to cross the border somewhere 600 kilometres to the south, are zero. But we decide to try. Twenty kilometres after Paris under two palm trees, on the border to nowhere, there's a new road check.

"To go to Bir Tarfawi, some 500 kilometres away, the road is good. But you have to ask permission to use the road," says the lieutenant in charge.

Twenty minutes later I have the commander of the region on the other end of the phone.

"Is this the way to Sudan?" I ask, after the initial greetings, as if crossing the desert were like going to the store to buy eggs.

"Sudan? Impossible!" the kind, but firm voice announces. "The only way is from Aswan, by boat."

Along with the first houses of Paris, Sahara, twenty kilometres back, a goat eats the pages of a book covered with handwritten notes. When we park in the main street a horde of children decide they're going to be our bodyguards. We just want to eat something and do our ritual tea and narghile before returning to the desert; today is a

Looking for a place to sleep at the White Desert, western Egypt.

contemplative day. But the street is shocked. The news that a foreign car has stopped in town spreads as fast as a dynamite fuse.

Two young men who speak fifty words of English take us hostage and riddle us with questions. People approach and every ten seconds someone yells *"welcome!"* even though sometimes the person who is welcoming you has already welcomed you three or four times. And even though you've told him you don't smoke, he's still offering you cigarettes.

"No thanks, Spain, no baby, Barcelona, yes, she is my wife, no, thank you, yes, Spain is good, *shukran,* smoking is bad, no, no TV, I'm sorry, she is my wife, Spain, Egypt *quaies,* sleep *siyyara,* yes we are married…"

It appears that this time I cannot be the Pope and simply raise my hand kindly through the windows of a Pope mobile. Now I'm the president of that imaginary country where everyone wants to shake my hand.

"Spain good, Barcelona football good, how much is a woman in Spain? She is your wife? You *quaies, siyyara quaies?* Give me your address, no telephone? Why? Al Andalus, yes, al Andalus good, she your wife?"

It's tremendous. We are prisoners of a band of fanatics.

It's the perfect little hell: constant repetition of the same routine, the same questions over and over again by the same people in a closed environment. The FBI, the CIA, Mossad or the KGB couldn't do better. We order a couple of falafel with salad and fries in a street stall and, just as we're getting ready to escape, the food arrives. These are the only minutes of peace, as we have our mouths full, nobody asks any questions. People come, watch us ruminate the potatoes, counting in silence as we chew thirty-two times, or arrive to forty, some whisper, and then leave. Our travelling circus really draws the crowds.

While we finish eating, the whole world becomes calm. Little by little the crowd disperses. Watching us eat is pretty boring.

With newly regained confidence, we make a mistake: we look for a place to smoke a narghile. Five youths who remain sufficiently far away start following us. The coffee shop is a mousetrap, a cage.

We sit down at a tiny table, they take five chairs and surround us, it's an ambush. We can't escape.

"Take a cigarette," repeats one of them.

"No thanks, I don't smoke cigarettes."

"Why not?"

"Because smoking is bad."

The TV is showing a football match between Kuwait and Bahrain. Zero to zero, Egypt isn't playing, nothing happens. And since watching us sit down and smoke a narghile is more interesting than what the players of Bahrain are doing with a ball, everyone forgets the TV and turns their chairs to watch us instead. Anna manages to escape into a book, but I am defenceless.

"Take a cigarette," says the same fellow seated to my right.

"No, I don't smoke."

"Why narghile yes but cigarettes no?"

"Why is she reading?" interrupts another.

"Because she likes to."

"The noise doesn't bother her?"

"Why does she smoke narghile?"

"Because she likes to."

"Women don't smoke narghile here."

There are perhaps thirty people in the coffee shop. Anna is the only woman.

"This is Ahmed, he's eight years old and works in construction."

"Ahmed, what about the *madrassa?*" I ask about his schooling.

"Lá, madrassa lá," no, no school, he responds.

"Children sit down and look at you," says one, "because you're different from what they see every day."

I get the impression he's excluding himself. He's older, speaks some English and sits with us not just for curiosity, but rather to keep us company.

I remember, loneliness is the Arab version of hell.

"I know," I reply. "It's the same reason we're here, because you're so different from us."

It's the only moment of reasonable conversation we have. After that, everything is noise, like the white noise of a television tuned to a channel that doesn't exist, a roaring motor, a vicious dentist who won't finish putting holes in your teeth.

The bartender pushes out the children who are occupying the aisle and other children replace them. Ten minutes later one of our kidnappers announces that he can play drums. The one next to him says he has an electric organ. Anna, supposedly absorbed in her book, looks at me sideways. I suspect the phrase which follows is *why don't you come to my place and dance for a while?*

At that moment, even though it's only 7:30 in the evening, my yawns are ostensible enough to politely decline the invitation and run faster than the Kuwaiti forwards. There are protests, we dodge a couple of interceptions and shirt grabs, *vamos, ¡vamos!,* but the decision of the referee is final, it's the end of the match. We flee into the desert.

I speed through the darkness down uneven dirt roads I know little about, and through some deep craters. The voices, the television, the mousetrap, the constant questions, still chase me and bounce off on the walls of my skull. I only stop when we lose sight of the lights and reflections of Paris, Sahara. I drive off the road and move between two dunes that glow under a crescent moon. Someone spent time spreading stars over the hard ground of the desert. The scenery, white on black, is beautifully alien. We want to be alone, but there is still no silence.

"Let's hide behind that dune," suggests Anna.

When we get out I open my mouth to let the noise escape into the night. Particles of chaos flow out in a tired sigh. My shoulders crumble to the ground without any strength, but remain attached only by flesh. Peace; deserts are the dry oceans of mainland, an infinite plain, beautiful to behold though less comfortable for the rest of the body during the day. That's why it's so lonely. Though...

"What is that?" asks Anna.

Something yellow lights up the dark horizon. Not too far away. It's a fire that's growing though, a fire? We're in the desert!

It's not possible. What was in that narghile?

Further back, another one lights up. In front of the first one, at some two hundred metres, we see the outline of a figure. I can't believe it. Even in the middle of the desert of Paris, Sahara, there's people. What's worse is that they've seen us. It seems impossible to escape today.

I've never liked nocturnal visits on the road. You don't know the intention of those who knock on your door after sunset, especially when you're in a remote place. I remember Turkey and the tiny Saddam Hussein who circled the van with a stick in the middle of the night. It's just you and them, humans, Martians or zombies, one or a hundred, you never know. In between there is only silence, the void, air.

Certainly, the tachycardia is on your side, next to isolation and doubt. Sometimes fear also remains, but that doesn't help much. How do you greet them? With a smile, some tea, a raised golf club? With a flare aimed at his chest? In a moment of danger, would you be able to fire, or would you submit yourself to fate?

Several shadows cross in front of the fires that glow on the near horizon. But they don't know us, we all gamble with surprise. They don't know if we're armed, if we're Taliban, fugitives or guardian angels. After fifteen minutes of waiting in the darkness we hear the whisper of voices approaching. They don't have lights. They're two figures, outlined in darkness, tar spots with fuzzy legs, armed with a stick or a shotgun. Not again.

Then I step forward with my old golf club, which I've never used to play golf, and start shouting.

"Salaam aleikum!"

Silence.

"Salaam aleikum!!!"

Silence. I take another step towards the figures that continue to come nearer and nearer.

"Salaam aleikum!!!!!"

My voice fades into the distance, but there's no answer.

"Aleikum salaam! Aleikum salaam!" comes the reply.

They're less than eighteen years old and they live here, in the middle of nowhere, where they've lit bonfires. They expected us to come over to them, a fire in the desert is a welcome signal, but we don't speak that language either. As we turned off our lights and remained in darkness they thought we were the bad guys.

Us, the bandits.

These guys are brave. After looking over the weapons, a wooden stick and a golf club, we agree to visit them the next day.

At dawn, as usual, the sky remains clear. Today there are no clouds on tour. When the sun rises some thirty degrees over the horizon it starts to get hot, the same as it does every day. Around us there isn't a single plastic bag tumbling in the breeze, there are no scraps of paper, no garbage. Paris or Baris, Sahara, is far away.

At ten in the morning a group of children dressed in rags greet us in their encampment. Their hands are covered in dust and their hair is matted with sand, but they're smiling. They're happy that we've fulfilled our promise.

Working in the desert destroys everything, hands, skin, eyes. The remains of their clothes hang on their shoulders with dignity. *I dress like this.* On one side is their house, a shed of plastic, wood and corrugated metal little more than a metre in height. It's ideal for a family of dwarfs.

Then a man appears from behind a high mound of chiselled stones. He's the only adult in sight, so he must be the boss. He's thin and displays such a huge smile that I can count the few teeth that remain in his mouth. He's the father of all these children, he's about forty, and according to Egyptian statistics in fifteen years he'll occupy his permanent place underground. I wouldn't give him more than ten; he seems destined to lower the national average life expectancy.

We sit at the door to their shed and we try chatting. They're all barefooted; the soles of their feet are leather tanned by stones and heat. The eldest son, the only one who has gone to school and knows some

English words, explains that the family works chiselling rocks. These rocks are used to build roads. They live here for thirty days, and then spend ten days at their home in Asyut, where their mother is waiting for them.

I look at their tools, looking for machines, and find nothing. The father and his sons break stones by hand.

While the youngest brother prepares tea, I spot the wooden branch which they were wielding last night. It's only slightly wider than a broom handle. I point at it and everyone laughs. They laugh even more when the boss, using sign language and broken words, explains that they also have a gun.

Before continuing on to Luxor we have to put some air in our tires. Our Chinese compressor is broken and the only nearby place is Paris or Baris, Sahara. The village garage is closed, though the neighbours, very friendly, assure us that it will reopen in five minutes. "No problem!"

A spectator brings the stereotypical international sign of friendship and joy: two frozen Cokes. Without doubt, their intentions are good. The rest drag out chairs from their homes. Anna engrosses herself in her book in the passenger seat and I patiently begin to answer the same questions from last night.

"No thanks, Spain, no baby, Barcelona soccer, yes, she is my wife, no thank you, yes, *Spani* is good, *shukran,* how much are women in Barcelona? And in Madrid? No money no, smoking is very bad, no, no TV, I'm sorry, she is my wife, *Spani,* Egypt *quaies,* yes we are married, sleep *siyyara,* al Andalus good? No telephone, why? Yes, she is my wife."

Everything is mixed, everything is confused. The price of meat at the Women's Market matters more than the price of oil. Nobody cares about what type of vehicle you use, the important thing is to know how much it costs. Then there is soccer, naturally, Barcelona or Real Madrid, the momentum which pushes the ball anywhere in the world causes eddies and currents which set in motion the winds of the planet. A smug man approaches and introduces himself as the tourist manager for the desert.

"Come to my house."

"Thanks, but we're just waiting for the garage to open to get some air for our tires. We have to move on."

A half hour later the garage remains closed. In the middle of the street ten chairs form an improvised circle, a containment wall that always returns the same questions, like a rubber ball. On the horizon more neighbours appear with their chairs. Everyone talks. Everything continues repeating itself. Through the window, two young men dedicate themselves to annoying Anna.

Suddenly, one of them goes towards the driver's seat, opens the door and sits behind the wheel. I get up, grab him by the arm, pull him out, and start the engine. The Manager of Desert Tourism tries to say something, that we should stay, that we're welcome, that it's lots of fun talking to us, that he would like to invite us to eat, that his son plays music, that he has an electric organ, that... his voice becomes distant as we move backward with our tires low in air, avoiding carts, donkeys and children.

There are more than two hundred and fifty kilometres of desert to Luxor. A desert of repeated questions, a desert of harassment, a desert of curiosity, of eyes, of voices, wonderful desert, desert, desert, desert!

In the middle of the desert, at last, we're deserted.

Nightfall. A policeman runs frantically waving his arms, his face transfixed in surprise. I've seen this scene in a movie. *"Watch out!"* he yells as his official cap flies off. Then a car bomb explodes behind him, and the guy goes flying towards you.

But no, this is not a film, this is just the third road check since leaving Paris or Baris, the policeman was distracted and wants to know where we're going. We're strangers. He asks, even though it's obvious, even though on the other side of the Nile are the houses of Luxor, the ancient capital of the Pharaohs.

"We're going to South Africa, is this the way?"

Apparently the city has two campgrounds, but in the tourist office they only mention one which is located in the garden of a hotel. The YMCA, the Young Men's Christian Association campsite, does not exist.

The little that I know is the YMCA is an association of young athletes, white and proudly Christian, descendants of Irish-Americans cut from the same pattern of immaculate perfection, military short hair and a smile out of a toothpaste advertisement from the 1950s. 'Village People', but without the gay angle.

I guess the tourism office must be right; its old peeling concrete walls look like a cemetery. On one side of the rusty iron gate the word CAMP has been hurriedly written with large irregularly painted letters. Inside are dozens of olive-skinned children that run around while their fathers play dominoes. They also slam the tiles on the table. At the far end is a camper with Italian plates that must have passed over the plastic tables scattered on the lawn that's seeded with garbage bags tossed along by the breeze. The television is blaring away at full volume above a wood fire, though nobody is paying attention to it. A good part of the straw roof of the bar, which appears abandoned, consists of a collection of holes. Today is the seventh of January.

"Salaam aleikum!"

"Merry Christmas!" replies one of the 15-year-old boys who pokes his head through a door while I recall that Christmas ended two weeks ago. "My name is Peter."

"Peter?" I don't understand a thing.

"Yes, and he is David."

"What became of Ahmed, Mohammed, Ibrahim or Ramadan? Peter is not an Arabic name. David, perhaps, could be."

"The thing is we're not Arabs. We're Copts. Christians. Are you Christian?"

"A bit," I respond. Then, they raise their wrists to show me a black cross tattooed on their veins.

The Greek Orthodox and Coptic Egyptians, all members of Eastern Catholicism separated after the Council of Chalcedon in 451 B.C., still count the days using the traditional Byzantine calendar. In other words, their calendar is offset by two weeks. Yesterday was Christmas Eve, and today it's Christmas again. The first year end of the new millennium, the first of the trip, proliferates in religious celebrations. In less than a month we've already had a Ramadan and two Christmases.

While I start to remember about this forgotten branch of Christianity, a short bald grandfather walks slowly through the barricade of chairs and tables.

"Ciao! Io sono Filiberto, Filiberto Spagnoli. Parlare Italiano? En Africa nessuno parla Italiano…"

Filiberto is 65 years old. Nine years ago he added up how much they would pay him when he retired and realised he'd already worked enough. He left his lifelong job in the basement of some ministerial bureaucracy, bought a backpack and went off touring the United States without knowing a word of English. He crossed into Mexico, then returned to Rome. With the same backpack he toured around South America and he spent three months in Rio de Janeiro, stretching out his tourist visa till the last day. It was difficult for him to leave the Brazilian woman who lit incense in his bedroom every night.

"She said she was Catholic, but she performed magic!"

After a while he left for southern Africa, then Asia, on voyages that never lasted fewer than nine months. He survived diarrhoeas, doubts, thefts, attacks from hungry fleas, forgetting cameras in taxicabs, elapsed visas, loneliness and the weight of a backpack until he was 62 years old. Then he bought an RV camper, and slowly went as far as roads permitted in the Sahara.

It's touching to hear the story of a grandfather who only speaks Italian and who had only travelled abroad once before giving up his regular way of life. The story of a man who suddenly noticed he was old and foolish. Of his frustration when he realised he had devoted his entire life to work and jumping between the beds of several women, yet never settling down with any of them. But the worst was the mocking which his family gave him when he announced that at the age of fifty-seven he was going to see the world.

"To see the world! Do you know how wonderful that is?" he exclaims excitedly. He pauses to reflect, he sighs, and continues. "They're the crazy ones. They only want money and even more money. They only think of money and everything they do is for money. The only real friend I have is now eighty years old. He was the only one who told me to leave, and if this was my desire that he preferred never to see me again.

The RV camper, his home, is parked out back.

"Do you know the only thing that I am missing?" He asks with a sad resignation.

"La patrona*?"

"Yes, *la patrona*." The travelling grandfather, incapable of communicating in any language other than Italian, remains quiet for a while.

Filberto had not stopped talking since he saw us. Hardly had he noticed that we could understand him that he started letting out all the words he had bottled up within him. He let them slip out with desperation, as if he had chocked on them and they were slowly rotting in his throat. He had to extract them before they broke down, before the worms arrived and they lost their meaning.

When we walk through the dark streets of Luxor, he advises us to go slowly. "Let's walk along that sidewalk, this one has many ups and downs. I drink only bottled water. *La diarrea non e buona.* When I left I had a larger stomach, now I only eat once a day and I'm developing a wonderfully fit body!"

The sellers in Luxor try to drag us towards their stores. Papyrus, plastic scarabs, pyramids that fit in the palm of your hand, pharaonic necklaces, earrings for Madame, books on the Royal Tombs in English, French, Italian, German, Spanish, Russian, Swedish, Catalan, Basque, Chinese, Japanese and even Arabic. The best food in town, *ganja my friend.* They pursue us with impossible-to-refuse offers or they stand in the middle of the sidewalk extending their arms towards their businesses in a futile attempt to change our direction. From the street

---

*The term "la patrona" is untranslatable. It refers in a literally to a wife, but one who rules in a greater matriarchal sense.

the horns of the old Peugeot 504's are only the prelude to voices that shout "ehhhh Mister! Taxi?" An artist waiting in front of the door of a souvenir warehouse turns theatrically, signals us with his finger and says in a firm voice, accentuating his words:

"I-know-what-you-neeeeeeed!"

Various men observe the street theatre and laughter, and without trying to foist us a piece of mummy or a Tutankhamen replica shout in unison: "I-know-what-you-neeeeeeed! Moneeeeey!"

When we return to the YMCA campground almost all the children have left. The party goes on and the adults continue punishing the domino tiles and talking in loud voices. The wind takes plastic drinking cups, bags and caramel wrappers out for a dance. Napkins hop up and remain afloat, each one is a Michael Jordan hoping that at some moment the laws of gravity will resume. Peter the 15-year-old Copt, who is no longer a child but not yet an adult, approaches to talk with Anna.

"Anything that you require just ask me. Gold, silver, antiquities, carpets, I can get anything!"

I move towards the bathroom between empty potato chip bags and more napkins that rise in small whirlwinds and eddies. A few metres

Old grafitti on an ancient temple in Luxor, Egypt.

from the door an invisible hand hits me in the face with a foetid odour, surprising for its intensity and unexpectedness. I enter the washroom covering as many orifices as possible, but I don't have enough hands. There must be a corpse, but what I find is much worse.

The mirrors are broken and the floor, with a fine layer of muddy water, leads to the only toilet, overflowing with all kinds, colours and sizes of human waste. I open the door to the shower and a souvenir the size of an obelisk stares back at me, standing upright in the middle of the cubicle. This place is full of landmines.

The scene is repeated in the women's washroom. The water from the broken faucet slides off the edge of the sink in rustic cascades towards the door. From the top of the stairs I look over the campground, thatched roofs full of holes, lawns sewn with plastic, and the fire beneath the television set. We're at war and I hadn't even realised it.

★

At ten past three of another heatstroke afternoon, a police convoy escorts two buses and three vans on the road to Aswan. From Luxor onwards, all foreigners who are not flying must join this armed convoy to protect them from would-be fundamentalist attackers. *We do this to guarantee your safety.* There is no other choice. There's no more freedom of movement.

At the head of the column an official truck establishes the rules:

1.   The average speed will be 120 kilometres per hour.

2.   The rules of the road are for queers.

Ten minutes after leaving Luxor I conclude that the police escort, which is supposed to protect us, could care less if we can keep up with them or not. They drive on the oncoming lane to pass cars, buses, trucks and donkeys without stopping, without caution, without reducing their speed, without fear. They're immortal.

Their strategy is to stick half their body out the window and make frantic hand gestures to vehicles to pull over, regardless of whether they're coming or going. It's the same gestures which you'd make if you suddenly discovered you had no brakes. For their passengers, policemen who lurch from side to side, shoulder to shoulder in the back seat, this is a hilarious game. The rest of the vans in the convoy, crammed with foreigners who are frozen in fear, play at getting a head-start on the strait sections, curves and bridges. It's like a video game, but in real life.

"They're crazy," exclaims Anna while she holds on to the door, the window, and her seat. "We're going to have an accident!"

Soon after, the buses disappear in the rear-view mirror. It doesn't matter. We travel through dusty villages at more than 100 kilometres an hour while children sit waiting for the column of vehicles to pass. Some day there will be a memorable accident and they'll be here to see it. If someone crosses their path it's their own reckless fault, and bad luck. Destiny hunts us.

This is the best example of Muslim fatalism: the future is written and no one has any power over what happens to their own lives. The future is in the hands of Allah and the only thing you can do to defend yourself is to put a sticker on your car that says 'GOD PROTECT ME.' Others have lettering that reads 'ME FIRST.' With these celestial shields they hit the roads.

I don't understand the reason for all this rushing while the slow beauty of the Nile prevails alongside us. Villages with adobe houses, old crumbling fortresses, women dressed in black, *fellahin,* carved hills where people lived a hundred years ago, donkeys pulling carts loaded with hay, buffalos and palm trees that continuously appear time and again. At this speed the only thing that doesn't change is the Nile. Everything else consists of fugitive faces, moving vehicles, fast landscapes, and life out of focus.

Halfway there, at another police checkpoint there is another column waiting for authorisation to leave in the opposite direction, towards Luxor. A man wearing a white galabiya, serious, obese and determined, approaches with a receipt book to charge the toll. There are no signs or posts or barriers that would suggest that they charge money here. There is nothing in English, or Arabic, nothing. We suddenly break into peals of laughter.

When you travel to another country, you imagine the rules of the game are similar to yours, but you never really know, you never know what is true and how much is a lie. The only thing you can do is get more time. At that very moment a military man passes by and sees us laughing, and he begins to laugh too. The toll is a ploy to get some money from us.

From here onward, the convoy has been reduced to the police car, another van, and us. The buses have disappeared. The landscape remains the same; fast. This time, however, when they reach 110 kilometres an hour, I continue driving at 90. Then the police car slows down beside us, in the opposing lane, and they start shouting.

"Faster! Your vehicle can go faster!"

"Yes, but the speed limit is 90 kilometres an hour!"

The policeman looks at me incredulously or indecisively. Then his partner accelerates and slowly distances himself.

Half an hour later, darkness swallows the asphalt.

The white lines which separate the lanes no longer exist and the road becomes covered with holes and vehicles that drive without lights to save on the cost of light bulbs. I have no idea how they manage it. Some only have their running lights on, but the majority have changed the connections so they can turn each headlight on independently and alternatively. Then the road becomes a fairground. Two powerful headlights turn on suddenly, then alternate from left to right, they get nearer and blind you, while an invisible vehicle passes next to you. Sometimes a drunk donkey appears, some lost soul, or wooden carts converted into mobile traps. A tractor, without lights and loaded with mountains of hay, crosses the road slowly.

A few kilometres later a couple of feeble lights approach from behind while passing vehicles. The large round headlights of a truck approach ahead.

The sudden braking force I apply to let the truck cut in front of us before we crash shatters what little is left of my sanity. The police, who had become accustomed to the monotonous 80 kilometre an hour speed, probably can't believe that we're the ones who are racing through the darkness wasting light bulbs. Or yes, perhaps they would; only a foreigner would use his high beams full-time.

I'm lost, and fearlessly I pursue a truck loaded with carefully balanced furniture; I hope the guy driving becomes nervous, is detained, or crashes against a palm tree. But no, my long beams don't hurt his eyes. He probably doesn't have a rear-view mirror.

When we arrive at Aswan I expect the police will say something, a reproach, a fine, an exaggeration, some new rule invented during the last hour. But there's nothing, momentary madness is not punishable in Egypt. It was written. Nothing, they simply disappear, swallowed by the empty yellow streets. Nothing, it's all the same. They abandon us.

★

In Aswan the same tourist tricks from Luxor are repeated, it's all from the same old school. Taxi drivers eager to take you to the moon, the merchants of shade assure you that you need a hat, traffickers of fake antiquities urinated on and buried in the patio of some house, salesmen selling spices at Japanese prices. Some of them can't control their laughter when they ask about our origins and Anna replies "Nubians, can't you tell?" The drivers of steaming horse-drawn carriages park in rows in front of four and five-star hotels where rosy coloured tourists pay in dollars.

In one corner is a child who's offering beer. He doesn't actually sell beer, but he knows where you can get a warm tin in this place where Prohibition turns the street into an open-air rehabilitation clinic. Everyone is looking for a way to make a living.

On the shores of the Nile an endless line of river captains wait with their feluccas, the traditional sailing vessel of Egypt.

"Three hours felucca, good price!"

"Sunset in a felucca?"

"Come in my friend! This is the best felucca!"

We eventually decide on a motorised collective boat, a survivor that floats amid asthmatic coughs and clouds of grey smoke to the island of Elephantine. The captain, whose facial skin is taunt and somewhat twisted as if he had skinned a mummy to dress up his own skull, reaches out and fills a glass with natural water with all sorts of minerals, collected directly from the Nile. Without a moment's hesitation, without thinking about happy streptococcus he downs the glass in one gulp; this always impresses foreigners.

What we really need is a larger boat, one that can take us to Sudan. Egypt is finishing, this is where all the sanctioned roads for foreigners end. You can only go to Abu Simbel by plane or on a tourist boat. The only official terrestrial border between Egypt and Sudan runs along the Red Sea, but it's closed to overlanders.

At the office of The Nile River Navigation Company, they say that we have to wait between one and many weeks until enough vehicles arrive to share the pontoon boat between Aswan and Wadi Halfa.

"Many weeks. It all depends on how many travellers arrive from Europe. Unless you want to pay 1,500 dollars."

But this time we're lucky. Another Overlander, an English truck converted into a passenger bus which covers the irregular route between London and Cape Town with intermediate stops, three continents, is a month behind schedule. And to think your boss used to give you dirty looks if you arrived twenty minutes late.

They intended to reach Sudan by way of Libya, but as they approached the border with Chad they learned about the fighting between some rival tribes. It was more than one of those traditional skirmishes that usually erupt to kill boredom. This was serious, and the road was cut.

Then they wanted to cross the desert from Khorga, in Libya, directly to Sudan, but the police withheld their passports. "A vehicle alone in this desert? Too dangerous! If you want to go to Sudan, you have to return to Egypt by the Mediterranean border post."

They didn't understand a word of Arabic, but when they hesitated at a crossing of confused tracks, a Bedouin with a perfect British accent appeared. "Can I help you?" The Libyan government was helping them find the road. They recovered their passports hundreds of kilometres later, at the border with Egypt.

Now they're in a hurry to get to Sudan and the driver, a scruffy, anorexic Englishman who sleeps in the cab, agrees to sell us a fourth of the pontoon.

★

★

★

★

"Do you think that in four years we'll be able to finish this trip around the world?" I ask as we move forward on the last kilometres of land, a burning asphalt road to the Port of Aswan.

Anna looks at me calmly. She doesn't say anything, but she suspects something. After six months of living together in four square metres she's beginning to correctly decipher the phrase that follows.

"What if we forget to go back?"

Her mouth remains closed but I know that she's insulting me. Her eyes say everything, *you bug.* A year ago we calculated that we'd be 3000 kilometres further south, *bastard.*

"I don't know, perhaps we should renounce our plans. We could continue to South Africa at a pace dictated by the road. We can abandon ourselves to the route, who knows, let the calendar be governed by the duration of the visas. We're traveling, right?"

The goal is Barcelona, probably.

The original plan to return to the life we left makes less and less sense every day we're away. I have proof, papers and photographs of a routine radically different from this slow wondering lifestyle. My memories become progressively stranger, more shocking. It's like the old Frankenstein confusion when he awakens after a few sessions of electroshock to discover that he doesn't need to obey orders, that he can be independent.

At the entrance to the port there are two types of soldiers: children with angry-warrior expressions wearing uniforms several sizes too big, and adults who inspect vehicles for weapons and antiques.

"Mummies?"

"No, just the two of us."

Inspections are always superficial. With a smile we repeat the usual spiel.

"Open up where you want, no problem. Here is the food, here is the clothing, here are the tools, here is the water, we sleep here and this is our narghile. No Tutankhamen."

"Smoke narghile?" A water pipe causes the same warm stream of sympathetic acceptance as a few words in Arabic.

I look at the military children, perhaps the plan is simply to live, not knowing where we are going until we've arrived. Perhaps we'll find another place. Perhaps it may be as simple as fleeing in one direction from the only destiny that is tattooed on us since the day we're born. It's funny, being born is a complaint, we're born crying.

Afterwards, we don't want to leave.

At the migration office, a man in an uniform with two stars, an eagle, and a button invites us to drink a coffee which he has to order three times while he inspects our documents. On the wall hangs an old map that shows Egypt and Sudan as only one country, when it was just one giant English colony. It wasn't that long ago. He checks our papers and stamps our passports but he keeps them. Everything is in order, but he won't let us leave the country until we have tried his coffee.

Through the window we can see the dock, Lake Nasser is an enormous huge bowl of grey soup with yellowish slopes that plunge into docile water. There are several small boats and a pair of worn-out barges moored at the shore. The activity is very Arabic, slow, quiet, nobody can take a stress leave here. The rate of cardiac arrest must be ultra-low. There's no rush.

At two in the afternoon we depart towards Sudan on a pontoon boat 25 metres in length called Heia II. The huge Aswan dam, built with Soviet support after Western outrage over the nationalisation of the Suez Canal, recedes in the distance but does not become smaller. It's impressive. The immense dreary mass of cement caused the sea level that extends below the surface of the Sahara to rise several metres. The actual cost of the flooding was paid by the Nubians, their houses and fortresses of adobe disappeared into mounds of diluted mud. People left, they abandoned their ancestral lands and migrated to the cities, to Sudan, or to the United States. Anything was better than starting anew, ploughing ungrateful sand, loose land that slipped through your fingers.

The Nile no longer exists in this invented inland sea. The sun shines and multiplies over the leaden surface of Lake Nasser. There can be no doubt, what I see appears to be another mirage. It is impossible that on these shores only more desert grows. There are no ploughed fields, wild reeds, or villagers carrying tools on the back of a donkey. So much good water and not a single square metre of green grass.

At port and starboard are uninhabited peaks of rock that barely breach the surface. Ahead appears another arid island with some forgotten temple on it. If I close my eyes I can tell that we're moving, I can feel it in the murmuring of the water, in the incessant purring of Siwa, the small blue boat that pushes our pontoon to the south. His heart, transplanted from a Scania truck, provides all the carbon monoxide that Mustafa the mechanic needs to live.

Standing on the deck, the black, porous and wrinkled skin of Captain Dahab is proof that we are approaching the heart of Africa. He must be close to retirement and his dark complexion contrasts with the white galabiya, whiter than the foam of the waves. His manners are soft, he speaks in a low voice, almost to the point of being a whisper. On his ship, orders are not yelled out. He looks at the horizon, signals something with his hand. Words are not necessary, everyone knows what he means.

A couple of hours after leaving Aswan we pause at the foot of a stone islet marked with a metallic bollard. It is impossible to navigate at night, the only electronic apparatus aboard the ship is a radio cassette player. From mainland the landscape is one of water and triangular peaks that emerge in isolation. There are no plants or animals, no cars, no people, no houses. Such desolation is absurd amid so much water. There is only one ruined hut at the top of another sunken hill, some hundred metres away. But there are no boats, the lake is empty.

★
★

At six thirty in the morning the voices of the sailors move into action. "Arabi! Arabi!" they shout calling the helmsman to attention. Our bed swings, and through the window of the van I see the sun stretching on the horizon and Captain Dahab, who extends his arm pointing south.

The South.

Departures are one of the few times when the entire crew works. While Arabi works the helm, Hassan and Ismail adjust the ropes which join us to our tugboat, Siwa on our port side. In the bow, Mofaq and Tarik measure the depth with a long stick while we separate slowly from the island. In the centre of the pontoon, next to the small cabin, Mule prepares the first narghile of the day with the same carbon used to heat water for the morning tea. The second day on board begins, the tugboat, the pontoon, a truck, a van, three foreigners, a captain and eight mariners.

There's not much to do if the lake is calm. It only requires steering towards south southwest while the propeller blades push under the water. That small degradation of the sonic landscape is the only thing that's out of place in this isolated and empty world where minutes last longer than anywhere else on the planet.

I look for crocodiles. They say the last one that lived between the Mediterranean and the Aswan dam was killed in 1891 by a British officer that must have felt proud of his accomplishment. I write. Now they can only be found on this side of the dam, towards the depths of Africa, towards Sudan. I smoke narghile with the sailors.

An old boat filled with passengers coming from Wadi Halfa passes some two hundred metres away while sounding its horn. It moves in slow motion, rigid, like a sustained note, like a giant cardboard model over fake waves in a puppet theatre. Everything else remains still, quiet, inert. Only the nearby water moves confusedly under the keel. I answer with our cow horn, Siwa also doesn't have a voice.

★

We cross the Tropic of Cancer at noon, as the sun continues flooding the desert with inflammable flashes. Under the only roof on deck, the sailors throw cards marked with stripes and peeling backs on the deck. Everyone appears to be over fifty. Captain Dahab must be sixty. The boat, almost a hundred. Mustafa wipes his hands on a rag covered in grease and he turns to study Mofaq's hand. He says something quietly and with a movement of his head he rejects the play. *Why are you playing those cards?* Our Arabic is still limited, but I understand everything.

Mofaq gets upset and looks up surprised at the humidity that has just fallen on his face. He wipes himself and is puzzled, *it's not possible that he had spit on me.* Then a gentle breeze from the west spatters him again with transparent drops. Feels like a gentle dew that has innocently been born on the surface of the water.

Captain Dahab looks at the clear horizon with furrowed brow and legs slightly apart. He forces his restless eyes to distinguish some small difference at the other side of the lake, where the Sahara continues. He knows what's approaching, though he would prefer to be wrong.

"It the wind of the full moon," he says in a louder voice, in his frugal English so we listen and understand, pointing to the two huge balls floating in the sky, a burning sun and an extinguished moon.

Suddenly the shore darkens. Half a minute later an invisible wave falls over us. The air, driven by a violent hand, shakes the deck and blows out the dust hidden in corners. The suspension of the van screeches with the sound of metal on metal. Mule throws the lit pile of carbon into the water and all the mariners run to secure the ropes which join the tugboat to the pontoon. Captain Dahab, who has not stopped looking to the east, to his Great White Whale, orders them to look for a protected cove on the mainland. Tomorrow we'll continue southwards.

★

On the third day Arabi settles into his chair to take the helm with his toes. His hands are busy, they're travelling across his teeth with a match. Two mariners argue, probably because there's nothing better to do. The maximum speed is about 15 kilometres an hour.

Even the waves seem uncomfortable with this monotony.

Yesterday, after taking shelter from the sandstorm, Mofaq, Tarik and Hassan went on a blind excursion into the desert. They returned two hours later covered in dust, with two old pistons and two rusty wheels.

Magic.

Today the wind is gone, the monster continued on its way to the east. I verify the fluid levels on the van. I adjust some nuts. Anna changes oil and fuel filters. I look at her black stained fingers checking the engine's belts, her hair wrapped in a coloured handkerchief.

She is not only my partner, she is also my friend, my comrade in arms.

I lie on the deck in the shade of the van and find a group of astonished sailors. They too have noticed.

★

Fourth day.

According to our GPS we're still about a 120 kilometres from Wadi Halfa and, at a speed of nine knots an hour, we'll be in Sudan at four in the afternoon.

Inshallah.

At eleven o'clock in the morning Abu Simbel appears. Captain Dahab diverts the ship to pass as closely as possible, only 50 metres from shore. I ask if he could stop for half an hour.

"If I stopped I'd go to jail" he replies. "I don't have a tourist license, and someone could turn me in."

We dodge some oil barrels that float towards Aswan. They're as empty as this timeline, as empty as the shoreline.

At one o'clock we arrive at the last outpost of the Egyptian police, the final frontier. There is no dock and a soldier gets his trousers wet to come aboard. With this heat they'll be dry fast. Behind him some officers arrive on a launch.

An hour later, when we retake the path towards the south, I ask Captain Dahab about Wadi Halfa.

"*Bukra,* tomorrow. *Inshallah.*"

"What will have become of Bahri?" asks Anna when the restless murmur of the sailors quiets to be replaced by crickets with throat problems. Mofaq, Tarik and Hassan snore together.

Bahri, our guardian grandfather with a captain's cap. Cappadocia. Houses carved in stone. Empty tombs, troglodytes. Do you remember?

Sitting on the gunwale, our legs are drawn to the water. The darkness is contagious, only the moon lights up the desolate landscape. Sudan is an ambiguous painting, blue burnt over black, *terra incognita* crouching on the shore.

Even the name causes turmoil, anxiety.

Africa is there, hidden like a lion with razor-sharp claws and an insatiable stomach. A true capitalist of blood, always ready to swallow hope and chew its bones. A continent dotted with dictators and armed conflicts where people learn to live with pain and share simple joys. Africa swallows everything, cannibalises everything. This is no longer tourism.

Real Africa starts in the centre of Sudan. Egypt is part of something else, an Arabistan which dawns in Asia and stretches along the shore of the Mediterranean to the Atlantic Ocean. The southern border is near.

On the surface of Lake Nasser Bahri's face appears with his captain's cap. Behind him are Orhan, Mehmet and his cross-eyed girls, heavenly and coal-coloured glances speaking new words without moving their lips. Along with Ziya and her missing sisters there is a key chain announcing Saudi America.

Further along there is the sad face of Nello, with his unbearable desire to forget about work and stay with his family in southern Italy. And there are Gareb and Mona, extraordinary, unique, "if we invite you to our house it's because we don't know you." And Ramadan and Christmas Eve on the same good night. All the Joes and Mohammeds of the world, God and Allah and Yahweh and Jehovah, and even a traveling Buddha who smiles at all the travellers that pass before his belly. Finally, a fat god! A god who doesn't suffer! A smiling sort of god!

I watch the lake, it hesitates.

We're crossing the waves now, and not smashing into them. The water is calm and melts into a uniform black mantle. We are arriving in Sudan, the commotion on land is enough.

For the first time I feel that it's still possible to live as we dream.

I return to the beginning of the story, a journey through the unforgettable roads of Babel. The day we declared our independence, the morning we renounced our security, the moment when all the continents reunited.

And there are colours, and hundreds of accents and distinct voices, all the lives on this planet, each speaking with their own words.

FIND ALL THE PHOTOGRAPHS FOR THIS CHAPTER AT
WWW.VIAJEROS4X4X4.COM

I went a little further,
*   then still a little further,*
*   till I had gone so far that I don't know how I'll ever get back.*
Joseph Conrad, The Heart of Darkness

The pontoon barge heading towards Sudan, on Lake Nasser, Egypt

Thank you. Gracias. Teçekur ederim. Shukran.

Nothing ever happens without a reason or without a cause. Even if it's you who has put blood, mud and ink on the table, there are always lots of people pushing to make this trip around the world a reality.

Martin, for example, that dread-locked Swiss with whom I travelled in Zimbabwe, who said I'd never leave my job to do the trip I had always dreamt about. With all my heart, Martin, thank you very much for the challenge.

Thanks to everyone who is in this book and to everyone who isn't. We've met so many lives, entered so many homes, shared so many dishes, and became confused in so many languages. The journey is sown with friends we'll never forget.

Thanks to author Gabi Martinez, who was the first to read the manuscript and assured and encouraged me to continue writing.

Special thanks to Joaquín Ayala, painter, musician and member of the Winter Harp Ensemble, who was so impressed with the book La Vuelta al Mundo en 10 Años: El Libro de la Independencia, that he decided to translate it into English for free, for the love of language and travelling. The result of two years of work is in your hands.

Thanks to our Vancouver, British Columbia friends who helped out in our discussions of words, sentences and meanings, especially to Christine Lambert and Lori Pappajohn.

Thanks to María José Baglivo in Argentina and the advertising agency El Laboratorio in Madrid, Spain for helping me with the cover design.

Thanks to all the companies that offered us their products during our journey. Thanks to Panama Jack in Spain for 13 years of boots and sandals, to Goal Zero for the Extreme Boulder solar panel we've mounted on our 4x4, to Mountain Khakis for their pants and to Ex-Officio for their shirts.

Thanks to everyone who helped rebuild our beloved house on wheels, La Cucaracha, after more than 10 years of travels on some of the worst roads in the world. Thanks to Scott Brady and Chris Collard of Overland Journal, to Mario, Clint and all the guys at Adventure Trailers, to Rusty Pérez and Alex Carvalho at AOE, to Florent Boisseau at CTC, to Gary Kardum at Mudrak, to Cristian Larrondo in Los Angeles, Trevor Graybeal at Pilot Rock and Fernando Rivero in Salt Lake City.

Thanks to all our Canadian friends in Vancouver who helped us with spare parts which were impossible to find in the Americas and for their work to ensure that La Cucaracha continues on the road. The end of the world is a place that is farther away than Deadhorse and Inuvik. Thanks to Laurentius Ersek, Richard Dagenais, Jessie Farsang, Paul Puleston, David Francoeur, Mardi Uy, Sabbir Sadeque and Butch Inducil.

But above all, many many many thanks to Christine Lambert (again!) and a big hug to Jay Willoughby, who welcomed us into their home for weeks and more weeks, worked on La Cucaracha and cared for it as if it were their own every time we flew back to Spain. You two are amazing.

Thanks to the bad times. Without them this overland trip would have been merely pleasant and boring.

Thanks to everyone that sent messages saying they liked the stories. Your words are my fuel.

And finally, and most especially, thanks to Anna for her courage and for going forward through the good as well as the bad, there being no shortage of the latter. Thirteen years ago I was convinced the trip would only be a long holiday, and upon returning, life would continue as before...

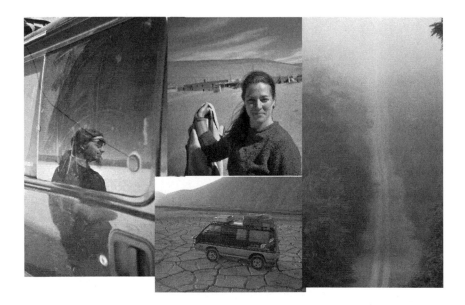

Pablo Rey was born in Buenos Aires. He arrived in Madrid in 1992 when Spain was in another bad recession. In 1996 he moved to Barcelona and in 2000 he rented his mortgaged apartment and moved into a 4x4 van with Anna Callau, his partner in adventures. The goal: to drive around the world through southern Europe, Middle East, Africa from north to south, America from south to north, and back to Barcelona via Vladivostok to Finisterre.

He has written articles for Overland Journal and Lonely Planet Magazine and has published three books in Spanish about his overlanding trips. Pablo is a former creative advertising writer, former illegal immigrant, an antique bottle hunter in ghost towns and one of many Argentinians from Barcelona, or Spaniards from Buenos Aires, with a leg in both continents.

Pablo and Anna still live on the road.